I Feel YOUR PAIN

A *7-Step* SURVIVAL GUIDE FOR EMPATHS, INTUITIVES AND HIGHLY SENSITIVE PEOPLE

NIKI ELLIOTT, PhD

Published by:
Transformation Books
211 Pauline Drive #513
York, PA 17402
www.TransformationBooks.com

ISBN # 978-1-945252-12-9
Library of Congress Control No: 2016958319

Cover Design: Vanja Dimitrijevic
Layout and typesetting: Ranilo Cabo
Editor: Marlene Oulton
Proofreader: Julie Clayton
Midwife: Carrie Jareed

Printed in the United States of America

I Feel YOUR PAIN

A *7-Step* SURVIVAL GUIDE FOR EMPATHS, INTUITIVES AND HIGHLY SENSITIVE PEOPLE

Disclaimer

The material presented in this book is for educational purposes only. The author does not intend to offer medical advice or in any way suggest that the exercises presented here are a substitute for treatment from a licensed mental health professional or physician. The purpose of this book is to offer information and support that the reader can use in a self-directed process of personal growth and spiritual development. The author and publisher cannot be held responsible for any outcomes that result from the use of the exercises or resources presented in this book. If you have any concerns for your well-being, please contact a licensed health care provider to support you.

Due to the sensitive nature of client privacy, all identifying details, including names and symptoms, have been changed. Other than editing for privacy, every effort has been made to provide accurate and reliable information to the reader. Please be aware that professionals in this field may have differing opinions and that change is always taking place in this dynamic arena.

Acknowledgements

As I think about how this book came into existence, I am in awe of the amazing hands of grace that led me to the right people, places, and events that allowed this story to unfold. Throughout my journey I have never felt alone, even in the midst of my most challenging experiences. I am forever grateful for everyone who has crossed my path and played even the smallest role in the unfolding of my destiny.

The completion of this project would not have been possible without the incredible people who support my work and live this message on a daily basis. Thanks to Shay Sayani and Nicole Pusateri for helping me document the foundation of my curriculum for the Innerlight Method, and for believing in this work when I had nothing to prove its efficacy. Thanks to Dr. Eileen Kenny, Juliette Hoffman, and my colleagues at the Healing Arts Center of Altadena, CA, for welcoming me into your community and helping me establish my private practice. This work could not exist in its current form without your endless support.

This book was lovingly shepherded by an amazing editorial and book promotion team: Mary Monroe, Amanda Johnson, Marlene Oulton, and Brita Richardson. Thank you all for recognizing the value of my message and for holding a high vision of this book with me.

The team at Transformation Books provided me with the loving support I needed to stick with deadlines and move past my fears of public exposure. I am forever grateful to Christine Kloser and Carrie Jareed for recognizing me as an emerging thought leader, and for inspiring me to rise up to the challenge.

Since I founded the Innerlight Method, I've had the honor of training more than three-dozen professionals and parents to access their intuitive gifts and practice energetic balancing as Innerlight Method Practitioners. I am grateful to every one of them for the lessons we learned together about how to share this work with larger audiences.

I am ever grateful for my home team: Charles, Amel, Élan, and Chaz. Thank you for being open to exploring this exciting and curious world of energy and intuition with me. Your support means the world to me. You are the reason I pushed past every obstacle in my path to develop this work. I love you and will always do everything in my power to make our home an energetically nurturing space.

And finally, to the empathic and intuitive children and families who have allowed me to guide them in a vulnerable area of life: thank you for trusting me to support and guide you in this unfamiliar arena. Each time I witnessed one of you achieve your highest potential it gave me more courage and more determination to develop the Innerlight Method. Your transformation and personal empowerment fuel my passion and give me the confidence to dream of a new world that embraces intuitive development and energetic healing as mainstream concepts.

TABLE OF CONTENTS

Preface

I Feel Your Pain

Sifting through a stack of old pictures, I came across a photo of an old friend. As I looked at the photo, remembering fun times from long ago, a sharp pain moved through my body unexpectedly.

Ouch! I clutched my heart as the pain landed in my chest. *What in the world is that?* I instinctively released the photo and closed the box I'd pulled it from, hoping that the pain would disappear. For the next several minutes, I attempted to distract myself by continuing to assemble my family photo album, but the pain didn't go away.

For the next few days, his face would float across my mind's eye and the pain would grip me again. It moved from my heart to the area under the right side of my rib cage. It would flare up each time he crossed my mind and then go away after about thirty minutes.

"*Call him...*" I heard my inner voice say.

No, I can't call him. I haven't talked to him in a really long time. He's going to think I'm crazy! I protested.

But the pain continued until I surrendered. I sat in meditation to ask what I needed to say when I spoke to him. In a flash, I understood that his liver was inflamed and that he needed to take immediate action to maintain his health.

Finally, I summoned up the courage to share what I heard, found his number, and called him.

"Hi, Adrian," I began, holding the phone to my ear and praying for the right words. *This man is going to think I'm crazy.*

"Hi, Niki. Long time..." he replied.

"I know. You've been on my mind lately and I wanted to reach out to see how you're doing."

"I'm okay," he replied half-heartedly. I knew it wasn't the full truth, but I wasn't ready to dive in just yet. He shifted the conversation away from being about him by asking how my children and family were doing. We played catch-up for several minutes before he said, "I feel like you called to say something."

"I did," I said, looking at the woman in the painting on my wall, hoping she would rescue me from this conversation. I took a deep breath to center myself. "I know it's odd to hear from me after all this time, but something reminded me of you last week, and you've been on my mind since." I paused, taking another intentional breath. "I've been learning something called energetic healing for a while now, and every time I think of you, I get this horrible pain in the area around my liver."

There was silence for a few seconds on the other end of the telephone line as Adrian digested my news. "My doctor just told me that I need to have my liver tested. How could you know that?" he finally responded.

"Like I said, I'm an energy therapist and something called an intuitive empath. I often feel other people's pain in my body and it doesn't go away until I give them the message I receive for them. Would you like to hear the message I've been given for you?" I was being as careful as I could be with him, because I knew this conversation was very unsettling for a man who had no previous experience with this kind of knowing.

"Yes...I want to hear it," he agreed.

"Okay, here's the message: If you cleanse for 10 days and work with some very specific essential oils, your liver will be okay and your doctor won't find any problems when they test you." The minute I said this, the pain I had been experiencing went away.

Silence. And then in a feeble voice he said, "I'll do it. I know something is not right in my body. I haven't had my normal energy level in a few months. I'll try it. Please tell me what to do."

I chatted with him for a few more minutes to explain the specific details of the message. When we got off the phone, I went to the health food store and put together a detox kit with the oils and instructions for the cleansing process and mailed it to him. He contacted me several weeks later to tell me that he had been to the doctor and they had given him a clean bill of health. More importantly, his energy levels were restored and he was back to his normal work schedule and exercise routine. He thanked me for having the courage to call him and admitted that he was a bit freaked out by the fact that I could feel his pain across the country.

Although I had frightened Adrian with the accuracy of my message, I was glad he felt better. Going out on a limb to help a friend felt worth the stress it had caused, and that night I prayed as I drifted off to sleep, *"Please God, teach me how to help people without feeling their pain..."*

In the past, if someone told you, "I feel your pain," you probably felt you were being heard and understood by a person who connected with you and cared about your suffering. But when *I* tell you that I *feel* your pain, I mean that I *literally* can feel your physical and emotional pain inside my body as if it were my own. At least, I used to—before I learned what it means to be an intuitive empath.

This may be true for you, too. You may feel people's pains and emotions as though they were part of your own physical experience. Perhaps you intuitively see images, hear sounds, or know thoughts or information that other people don't access. You may be highly sensitive to energy and the environment around you. Whatever *your* unique expression of intuition or energetic sensitivity is (and every individual is different), your gift comes with a special set of challenges and benefits. After years of exploring my own intuitive gifts and specializing in energy balancing for intuitive adults and children, I wrote this book to share the techniques that have helped me, and my intuitive clients, to overcome the challenges and to thrive by using their intuitive abilities with intention and discernment.

I believe we need to consider empathic overload as a viable part of assessing every aspect of wellness, including mood, learning, behavior, and physical health. Some energy balancing specialists believe that the majority of emotional, mental, and physical ailments are actually rooted in energetic imbalances.

We are all connected, and everything and everyone leaves an imprint on our energy field. In fact, our interconnectedness is the core of who we are. If you are intuitive or energetically sensitive, you are more likely than most to be challenged by empathically blending with people and your environment, which is essentially taking on or absorbing other people's pain, joys, excitement, and fears.

Unfortunately, we are not taught to take care of ourselves energetically.

We understand the need for good physical hygiene. We shower, wash our hands, and brush our teeth. But we aren't taught that as energetic beings we have an energy body that requires as much care and attention as our physical body does. When we become aware of our intuitive nature and our energetic body, we can learn how to cultivate our gifts, practice energetic wellness, and thrive. That's when we are able to fully shine our unique passion, talents, and genius on the planet.

Imagine if every human being were able to fully utilize his or her intuitive potential! What would the world be like if we received training in the appropriate and balanced use of intuitive gifts? How many of our global problems could be solved, bringing us closer to experiencing heaven on earth? What would our world be like if we intuitively knew the truth of who we are and what we need? How would our personal and international relations be improved if we lived and acted from our intuitive awareness of the highest truths, rather than getting caught up in fears, worries, and drama from the media or from others around us?

Imagine how our schools would be different if we taught our children to engage their intuition as part of the learning process. Picture how our health care system would be different if we included intuition as part of the process for patients and practitioners. Even our family lives would be dramatically altered if we honored and cultivated intuitive wisdom at home.

If you were fully "you" and maximized all your intuitive gifts and talents, how would you be different? How would your world be different?

If you think you may be (or know you are) an empath, intuitive, or energetically sensitive person, *I Feel Your Pain* is a message of hope and empowerment. You are *not* broken. You are gifted and you *can* learn to take control of your gifts and your life. If you are a minister, doctor, nurse, coach, therapist, teacher, or other helping professional, you will learn to stop absorbing the pain of others and integrate a new intuitive dimension into your work.

Your intuition is a powerful—perhaps the most powerful—part of you. Isn't it time you got to know it better?

Introduction

Going Down the Rabbit Hole

The minute I stepped into the checkout line and stopped my busy thoughts about menu planning and comparison-shopping, a creeping anxiety came over me.

My breathing became shallow. My heart began to race. I clutched the edge of my cart with excessive force as I bent over to put my groceries on the conveyor belt.

Ouch. Suddenly, my knee began to hurt. It was the fifth time in the past few weeks I had been overcome with random physical pains that I had never experienced before. *What is happening to me?* I thought, as I continued putting items on the counter.

It wasn't an easy question to answer. It had only been three weeks since experiencing one of the most painful events of my life—delivering my first child, a stillborn daughter named Noelle. It was every parent's worst nightmare. When I thought back on the experience, I recognized that I'd had a subtle advanced knowing that I wasn't going to be bringing her home from the hospital. I had unconsciously put off doing the usual things new moms do to prepare for their babies. I didn't beg my husband to help me assemble her crib or wash the barely used baby clothes that had been passed on to me from friends. Some part of me knew, but didn't know how I knew, that Noelle wasn't coming home with us.

And now, weeks later, in addition to almost unbearable grief, I was constantly finding myself overwhelmed with anxiety and weird pains that would come and go whenever I went out in public.

Something is wrong…really wrong…and I have no idea what to do.

At that time, I certainly had no idea that what was happening to me was actually a good thing, even though it felt horrible. The trauma of the childbirth and distress of losing a child had cracked me open energetically…and all of the intuitive gifts that I had been suppressing since childhood began flooding me with full force, making it impossible for me to ignore them any longer. There was no turning back.

Remember how Alice fell down the rabbit hole and found Wonderland? Yes, some of it was wonderful, but some of it was frightening. When we go "down the rabbit hole" of our intuition, we can feel a lot like Alice—disoriented, confused, and sometimes terrified. When I first became aware of my intuitive abilities, I did everything I could to climb back out!

There are many ways that people fall into the rabbit hole. Jill Bolte Taylor, author of *My Stroke of Insight: A Brain Scientist's Personal Journey*, fell down the rabbit hole when she had a massive stroke and the left hemisphere of her brain shut down. She relayed her blissful right-brain experience of nirvana in her bestselling book, and her story became the first TED talk to go viral on the Internet.

She is just one of many scientists and academics whose lives and careers have been reshaped by intuitive awakenings and abilities. Harvard neurosurgeon Eben Alexander, who wrote *Proof of Heaven: A Neurosurgeon's Journey into the Afterlife*, was a skeptic who never expected to go down the rabbit hole until a near-death experience changed him forever.

Barbara Brennan was a NASA physicist before she became an energy healer and founded a global training institute for energy healing professionals. Judith Orloff, MD, is a psychic and empath, as well as an Assistant Clinical Professor of Psychiatry at UCLA. She is a widely respected pioneer in the field of energy awareness, and synthesizes traditional medicine with her knowledge of energy, intuition, and spirituality. Each of these gifted people, and many more, have changed hundreds of thousands of lives—millions even—because they have chosen to blend the power of their intellect with the power of their intuition.

One of our greatest fears is that developing our intuition will set us apart from people who are intelligent and accomplished. The truth is that many of the world's most intelligent and accomplished people are in the rabbit hole with us!

There is a powerful spiritual awakening underway today that is attracting people of all backgrounds, including those who have been classically trained in the sciences—people that we might expect would dismiss intuition as hocus-pocus.

As an academic and an educator, I never expected that I would one day be teaching and writing about intuition or energy medicine. But after going down the rabbit hole myself and working with many other intuitive children and adults, I now wholeheartedly believe that integrating the spiritual and the academic, the intuition and the intellect, is the only way to achieve our full human potential.

Through the seven steps in this book you will learn to understand, manage, and integrate your intuitive nature into your life and work. You will learn how to:

- See your abilities as the divine gifts that they are, rather than a curse to wish away
- Recognize and avoid empathic blending that can be detrimental to your well-being
- Avoid unnecessary medication and restricted living

- Identify the type(s) of intuition you have
- Trust the intuitive information you receive
- Control your intuitive faculties to fit smoothly into your life
- Develop your intuitive skills
- Balance your intuition and intellect for harmonious living
- Integrate your intuition into your life for the fullest expression of your potential

On Your Own in a New World

Unfortunately, most of us are not prepared for what we find when we first begin having intuitive experiences. In an ideal world, a teacher, mentor, guru, or medicine man would guide the development of our intuitive faculties. Our community or tribe would respect and honor our abilities. We would be taught discernment, healthy energy boundaries, and how to best use our gifts. Our tutor would ease us through mis-steps and make sure that we had appropriate physical, mental, and emotional purifying, detoxing, and lifestyle habits to keep our intuitive channels open and clear. Under expert guidance, we could grow to our highest potential.

Does that sound like your experience? It certainly wasn't mine!

Most of us didn't ask for it, weren't prepared for it, and knew no one who understood what we were going through. We feared for our mental and physical well-being, and may have been afraid to speak up for fear we would be ridiculed, or lose a job or relationship. In some environments, talking openly about intuition can be as highly charged as talking about your sex life in public!

Usually we go down the rabbit hole alone and are on our own until we can find teachers and a community to help us. That is not always easy in a culture that can view intuition as a myth, superstition, naiveté, "devil's work," etc. For all the people who are actively developing their abilities today, there are likely many more who just don't have the support to do so.

As mentioned earlier, we sometimes stumble into our own intuitive ability through illness or near-death experiences. It can also happen through physical accidents. Famed psychic Edgar Cayce, for example, sustained a significant head injury before his intuitive faculties were opened.

Other common catalysts are severe emotional traumas, such as the death of a loved one or childbirth (which may be why we think of "women's" or "mother's" intuition). Sometimes as children, our intuitive abilities open prematurely as a survival mechanism if our parents have addiction issues, put us at risk of sexual, emotional, or physical abuse, or are chronically ill or otherwise unstable in their caregiving. While this is most often the case (a safety mechanism), on occasion children are born with an insatiable curiosity about the world, and since their intuitive channels are innately wide open, this is how they "sense" it. Psychotropic drugs such as ayahuasca (an Amazonian plant mixture capable of inducing altered states of consciousness), can also open up our intuitive or spiritual awareness.

The circumstances that open our intuitive awareness are different for every individual, just as the abilities themselves are varied. You may find you are sensitive to the energy of people or environments, experience altered states or other dimensions, communicate with the deceased, become aware of others' pain or illnesses (the gifts of a medical intuitive), or become aware of events in the future, just to name a few. The world of intuition is vast!

I believe there is a spiritual imperative for each of us to evolve. Throughout our life, the Divine Spirit within us rises up and seeks opportunities to bring us into our intuitive awareness. We may not plan to go down the rabbit hole, but one way or another the rabbit hole finds us.

Two Steps Forward, One Step Back

Once I realized I wasn't getting out of the rabbit hole, I began to study Reiki and learn more about energy. I met people who understood energy and intuition and they encouraged me to develop my gifts. I went on to study Kundalini yoga, Theta healing, and several more energy balancing systems and found that each had something magnificent to offer. I experienced a lot of meaning, pride, and joy in learning to help others with my intuitive gifts.

I realized that although I had lost my beloved Noelle, I had opened up to these gifts, which I could use to help others. Increasing numbers of people that I worked with were healing emotionally and experiencing powerful psychic transformations after our sessions. There was only one problem—I was getting sicker. I was taking on the energy of the people I worked with. It got so bad that after a couple of years I had to stop. At that point, I was the mother of two young daughters and I just couldn't be in bed with empathic sickness all the time.

Even though I had great instructors, no one taught me what I needed to know about being an empath. Nobody talked about the dangers of embodying the pain and disease of others, or how to distinguish what was mine from what belonged to others. Because I didn't have the training I needed, I had to stop doing energy work altogether.

For four years my intuition kept urging me to listen and I kept begging for my intuitive gifts to go away. I didn't want people to think I was crazy. Some of my friends and family were shying away from me, afraid that I might suddenly know their secrets or read their minds. I prayed, *"Please take this away! I hate it! I just want to be normal."*

In no uncertain terms, I wanted out of the rabbit hole.

Finding My Focus

I was working as a school administrator in a public charter school and watching the children at school line up for their medications when I heard an inner voice say, *What if what is going on with some of those children is not a mood or behavior problem like everyone thinks? What if they are energetically "sick" like you are?*

It was that voice and that question which made me begin my intuitive work again. I was an educator and loved working with children, so I decided I wanted to explore working with energetically sensitive children.

In order to do that, I needed to get healthy myself. I knew I couldn't help others if I was feeling sick all the time. I started to make a list of *my* demands for working with my intuitive gifts. I wanted to make the rules rather than be a victim of circumstance.

Then synchronicities started happening. I started reading about children and energetic sensitivity. The books, articles, and resources I needed came to me. People started to ask me to do energy work and I asked them if I could help with their children.

Energetically, I asked the children I worked with what they needed from me. Those children helped me piece together the energy technique that ultimately became the Innerlight Method. The more I (and those I trained) worked with children, the more success we observed.

In 2011, I leased a room to practice energetic work and launched Innerlight Sanctuary to help intuitive, empathic, and highly sensitive children and their families. Although my initial focus was on children, their parents quickly began to ask for help, too. Soon I was working with both children and adults, teaching them how to dial their gifts up and down, have more control over their intuitive faculties, and trust their abilities.

In addition to parents, I began teaching therapists, social workers, psychologists, educators, child care providers, and other professionals so they could avoid absorbing the energy of people around them and learn to help the intuitive adults and children with whom they worked. I helped them feel healthy and vibrant again without the burnout and the energy absorption sickness that I knew so well. I trained people to bring energy balancing to Pasadena City College, and also presented energy balancing information sessions to the staff at Kaiser Permanente, one of the major health care providers in California.

In fact, my first major presentation on energy work took place at the ADHD Clinic at the Los Angeles Kaiser Permanente Hospital on Sunset Boulevard where I was born, and where I had lost my baby, Noelle. I was nervous about bringing my message of energy balancing into a conventional clinical setting, but they were an engaged audience. They were interested in exploring alternative options since many of their patients' families wanted to explore other possibilities for treatment before putting their children on medication.

The presentation and the social worker's receptivity exceeded every expectation. As I drove home that day, I started to cry. I finally understood both why I had been born and why I had lost my baby. I experienced closure on the loss of Noelle. I realized that without that loss, I would never in a million years have found this path. It felt like a full integration of my journey: the loss and the grief; the challenges when I was feeling crazy; the struggle to learn it all; and the development of a method to help other intuitive people.

I cannot explain the unimaginable grief of being told your baby is dead, but as I began my new career, I made peace with it as I realized a clear and renewed sense of my purpose in life.

With my PhD and other degrees, I thought I was going to build charter schools for special needs learners and serve as a teacher and administrator. Instead, my intuition led me to a new mission—to strip away the stigma of "hocus pocus" and transform the way we integrate intuition and energy awareness into mainstream life.

It was a painful journey. There were times I thought I was dying, and times doctors were telling me I was a hypochondriac, but today I wouldn't trade my experiences. Every time someone tells me I have changed their life, I know I would go down the rabbit hole all over again.

In this book, I'm going to share the seven survival strategies that brought me from my initial struggles as an empath with illness and paralyzing anxiety, to the point where I no longer feel your pain unless I *choose* to, such as when you are on my treatment table for an energy balancing session. That's right! No more surprise episodes in public places! No more trips to my doctor with mysterious health problems I have absorbed from other people. I use my intuitive faculties *only* when I intend to use them.

You too can have dominion, authority, and control over your intuitive abilities. Your gifts should not be dragging you by the tail, interfering with the life you want to live. When you know how to manage it, intuition is a blessing and a birthright, not a curse or an obstacle to be overcome.

I have met and worked with so many people—adults and children—whose daily lives have been impaired by their intuition and energetic sensitivity. Highly sensitive children often have difficulty in school, where they are sometimes misdiagnosed and incorrectly medicated. Adults can become so used to suppressing their gifts that they often don't realize how much they have limited their activities, such as avoiding crowds, for example, or medicating themselves to manage their anxieties. Empathic people who work in helping professions get burned out from absorbing the energy of their students, patients, and clients, and sometimes have to give up the work they love to survive.

When intuitive people learn to recognize, manage, and develop their capabilities, they blossom with newfound genius. This is the beauty of balance—intuitive people naturally have strong right-brained abilities, but don't know how to integrate them into their lives, especially in a seemingly left-brained world that reinforces the value of logic and intellect. I tell clients, "Inner balance equals outer brilliance."

When children learn to understand, control, and make creative use of their intuitive gifts, they do better academically.

They begin to discover new talents and possibilities. Adults who recognize and develop their intuitive abilities instead of denying or suppressing them often begin to excel in their careers and find new meaning, passion, and joy in their lives.

If the world is so logical and left-brained, how is it possible that intuitive people can excel at school and at work? The surprising truth about intuition is that it is every bit as valid as the intellect when it comes to creating success and fulfillment in life. Academics use intuition all the time, as do inventors, business moguls, and many world leaders.

Steve Jobs said, "Have the courage to follow your heart and intuition. They somehow already know what you truly want to become. Everything else is secondary."

And years ago, Albert Einstein said, "The intuitive mind is a sacred gift and the rational mind is a faithful servant. We have created a society that honors the servant and has forgotten the gift."

Jobs and Einstein knew that intuition and genius go hand-in-hand. Although the world may not understand intuition as well as it does intellect (yet!), there is absolutely no doubt that the power of intuition is enormous. If we surrender to our lack of understanding and shy away from our intuitive gifts, we are leaving our genius potential on the table.

We think highly successful people like Jobs and Einstein achieved what they did because of how smart they were. In truth, it may have been their intuition, not intellect, which made the difference. Einstein attributed his discoveries to his ability to access the realms of intuition and imagination. He stimulated his creativity with four activities—biking, bathing, napping, and playing the violin. He knew what he was doing (well, he was Einstein!) because movement, water, rest, and music are highly effective strategies for helping us connect with our intuition.

We have a tendency to think that intuition and intellect are at odds with each other, when in truth they work beautifully together. Our intuition is often associated with the feminine part of our nature, and intellect with our masculine nature, so perhaps it isn't surprising that our society is biased toward what we think of as intellect.

But this imbalance is rapidly shifting as more people—men and women alike—recognize and develop their intuitive abilities. Just as the masculine and feminine complement each other when in balance, intellect and intuition can harmonize to create a whole that is far more effective than either quality can be on its own.

We don't think of Einstein as "New Age-y," or "woo-woo," or "out there." We recognize him as a genius! What if you restored and activated your intuitive capacities as Einstein did, and applied them to the areas of your life where you have talents, interests, and passion? What "E = MC-squared" breakthrough is waiting for you in your life?

Developing your intuitive gifts is not about taking yourself up to a mountaintop where you will have enlightening experiences all by yourself (unless that's what you want to do). Mastering your intuition can actually take you more fully and deeply into your everyday life, where you can create more success and happiness for yourself, your loved ones, and the communities in which you live and work. The world needs you to be at your intuitive best so that your new perspectives, ideas, and inventions can enrich us all, just as Einstein's discoveries have enriched our lives.

Every day I meet people who have learned to trivialize, ignore, or bury their intuitive capacities. It may be that most people have become accustomed to setting aside their inner voice of wisdom. We usually haven't been taught how to nurture and trust that voice, so naturally we distrust or even fear it.

But for people who are highly intuitive or energetically sensitive (*e.g.*, "right-brained")—and as much as 30% of the population is—denying our intuitive nature can create anxiety along with a host of other mental, emotional, and physical problems.

My job is to catch you when you fall down the rabbit hole. I teach people not to fear their gifts or believe the myths that cause them to feel ashamed or afraid.

With the help of the seven steps in this book, you can experience the higher vibrations of your intuition without blowing out your nervous system or experiencing other symptoms of energetic overload. You can choose when and how you fully integrate the genius of your unique intuitive gifts into your life to fulfill your soul's highest purpose.

Let's get started!

1

Step One: Face Your Fear

Embracing the Truth About Intuition

"Please help me! He's going to kill me!"

I scanned my environment to find where the voice was coming from. It was three years after the loss of Noelle, and I was pregnant with my third daughter, Élan. My husband and I were enjoying a Jill Scott concert when I heard a woman's voice in my head, saying, *"Please help me! He's going to kill me!"*

I tried to pay attention to the concert, but just became more anxious. *Am I having a mental breakdown?* I wondered.

Then I heard the voice say, *"I am right in front of you."*

I saw the back of her head in the row in front of me and a man seated next to her, his arm draped loosely around her shoulder. At that time, I didn't know what clairaudience was. I only knew that I couldn't enjoy the concert—and I love Jill Scott!

So I asked her silently, "What am I supposed to do?" and I heard her ask me to pray for her to have the strength to get away from the man next to her. I started to pray for her, just to make the voice go away.

I wasn't exactly sure what kind of prayer I was supposed to pray. Intuitively, I prayed for the woman's forgiveness, strength, safety, and release. I prayed for her to know how beautiful she is to God. But as I prayed, I noticed that the man next to her started to tighten his grip on her shoulder. I watched her squirm in her seat as he pulled her tighter.

At the time, I didn't know what I know now—that when we do energy work to cut cords or disconnect our energy from a partner, the partner can feel the shift happening and will often react negatively. In that moment, all I could see while I was praying was his clenching her tighter, and her pulling away.

I realized that I didn't know what I was doing or how my energetic involvement was impacting the couple. I became nervous and stopped. As nausea washed over me, I worried about the safety of the baby growing in my belly. When I started to cry, my husband asked, "Is someone here making you feel sick?"

I nodded my head and pointed to the woman in front of me.

"Let's go," he quickly replied.

As we walked away from our fifth row seats, I silently wondered if I would ever be able to enjoy public events again. I didn't know it then, but I was going to be guided to all of the skills, tools, and teachers I needed to manage my gifts, rather than feel like I was a victim of them.

You Are Not Crazy

One of the most common fears for energetically sensitive people is that their intuition is a sign of mental or emotional instability. Let me reassure you that intuition *does not* make you crazy! If you have not acknowledged your intuitive nature and addressed its role in your life, what you probably are is exhausted from intuitive overload.

Recognizing your intuitive nature may help you understand why you:

- Feel drained, fatigued, or depleted
- Find it difficult to be in a crowd or in other triggering environments
- Hear voices, see images, or have dreams that keep you up at night
- Feel burned-out from the emotions of people around you at home or at work
- Feel pains that have no apparent cause
- Question how to handle intuitive information that others may not know
- Struggle with how to integrate your intuition into your life and career

Balancing Intellect and Intuition

I have always highly valued the power of intellect and education. In fact, my passion has always been education. My academic career began with a bachelor's degree from UC Berkeley in African American Studies. I was interested in studying the sociology of education. I knew there were educational inequalities for black students who often weren't perceived to be as intelligent as other children.

My bachelor's thesis was about the culture of poverty theory and its impact on the educational opportunities available to low-income children of color. I decided that I wanted to build schools that would help non-traditional learners thrive, so I went to Teachers College, Columbia University, in New York City. There I earned a master's degree in Urban Schooling and began to teach fourth and fifth graders on the East Coast.

As a teacher, I soon noticed that I would often be assigned to the very bright children of color who had behavior or anxiety problems—children the other teachers didn't know how to reach. I fell in love with these exceptional, but distressed children, and developed a record of success in working with them.

I wanted to help create learning environments where these children could thrive. I was still interested in the issue of inequities. I noticed that white children with challenges were often perceived to be smart and bored. They were referred to gifted programs, while children of color were referred to programs for behavioral problems and not given access to higher educational opportunities. I was also curious about the general population of exceptional children who were often highly sensitive.

When I came back home to California, I won a Spencer Fellowship to study Urban Schooling at the UCLA School of Education. There I earned my PhD in Education with emphasis on charter school design. My goal was to build alternative, holistic environments that would give bright but distressed children the opportunity to learn. I began to work as an educational consultant, helping people build and design charter schools, and ultimately I became the founding board president of Aveson Charter School in Altadena, California.

Aveson was where I first began to integrate energy balancing into the educational curriculum for sensitive and gifted children. As word of my success travelled, I opened the Innerlight Sanctuary in Pasadena, California, so I could offer the benefits of energy balancing to more children and their families.

Sometimes those benefits came in unexpected ways. For example, a woman called me because her husband, a Vietnam War veteran, was having night terrors. He could hardly get out of bed, focus, or be present with his family because he was so affected by his war experience. I suggested he see a specialist in Post-Traumatic Stress Syndrome (PTSD), but she said he was already seeing a psychiatrist.

At that time, I was only seeing children in my practice, so I was reluctant, but I agreed to see her husband. As soon as the energy session began, I could feel that he was very receptive and desperate because it was breaking his heart that he couldn't enjoy everyday life with his family.

His energy field felt like it was being stabbed with porcupine needles. I could feel the stabs in my body and I could see him energetically tangled up like a dolphin caught in a fishing net. I energetically asked him what he needed me to witness so he could have relief from the turmoil.

He showed me that he was empathically blended with the energies of what his fellow soldiers experienced in the war—all the passion, sorrow, anxiety, and fear. He was one of the most empathically intuitive men I have ever met, but he had no mechanism for clearing out the extreme emotions and experiences of battle. He asked me to help him untangle energetically from everything he had experienced, so I watched the shifts in his field as he untangled himself. (In the Innerlight Method, the client, rather than the practitioner, clears and balances their own energy field while the practitioner guides them.)

The next day, he called to tell me he was able to sleep that night for the first time in years. After three sessions, he was out of bed, gardening, driving, and fully participating in life, including taking the medications prescribed by his psychiatrist.

As if that wasn't remarkable enough, there was a bonus effect of the work he had done to clear his empathic energy. The veteran and his wife lived with their daughter and granddaughter. He was very attached to his granddaughter, and they hadn't told me that she also had screaming terrors at night. After my first session with her grandfather, the child's night terrors also stopped. She had been absorbing her grandfather's empathic blending energy. They were both empathic intuitives and now they could both get a good night's sleep! Addressing empathic imbalances changed the quality of life for the whole family.

The more people I helped, the more my gifts opened up. As I worked with children and adults, studied various energy medicine modalities, and learned to master my intuitive abilities, I came to see how I could creatively integrate my gifts into my life and my work. I found unexpected ways to balance the "left-brained, masculine," intellectual side of my nature with the "right-brained, feminine," intuitive side. Remember: Inner balance brings outer brilliance!

You, too, can develop your intuition, cultivate balance in your life, and create brilliant new possibilities, solutions, and directions in your life. But in order to do that, you must identify and overcome your fears about your intuitive gifts.

Lesson One: Your Fears are Mostly Myth

Do you know that acronym for F.E.A.R.: *False Evidence Appearing Real*? It turns out to be especially true for our fears related to intuition. When I teach classes, I ask my intuitive students to list their fears about expressing or developing their intuition. One by one, we determine if each fear is actually true or simply a belief. Most everything on the list gets crossed off as a perception rather than a reality.

Do you know what your fears are? You might want to make your own list of what you think could happen if you allowed yourself to trust your intuitive wisdom, or you "came out of the closet" with your intuitive gifts. Then ask yourself how true your fears really are.

Here are some of the more common myths that intuitive people believe. I know because I've heard them repeatedly and I believed some of them myself.

Myth: Intuitive or psychic abilities are "dangerous."

Truth: Intuition of itself is neutral, neither "good" nor "bad." It just is. The real question is, "For what purpose is intuition being used?" Is it being used to influence, manipulate, or control outcomes or people? Or is it being used for higher guidance, wellbeing, and healing benefits?

Think of your intuitive abilities like water. Water just… is. If you do not have enough water, you'll die of thirst, but if there's too much, you can drown or your house can be washed away in a flood. The same substance that is absolutely essential can also be destructive. Or think of fire. It is essential and life-sustaining when it warms you, cooks your food, and keeps you from freezing. It is also absolutely dangerous if it consumes you or burns down your home.

The same is true of your intuitive abilities. They can be transformative and affirmative, or the cause of stress or harm to yourself and others, depending on how they are used and with what intention. We teach our young children to be afraid of jumping into the pool without supervision, or touching a hot stove. But as they grow, we teach them to swim and to cook. We are meant to grow out of these fears as we learn to act responsibly. You're no longer afraid of fire or water because you have learned how to use them safely.

With your intuitive abilities, you have to make the commitment to understand how they work and exercise proper discernment. Some of my students have voiced fears that expressing their intuitive abilities will ultimately lead to them jeopardizing their mental health or going crazy, attracting dark energies or bad spirits, manipulating others, or causing harm. No wonder they don't want to recognize their skills! But that seems a little like not drinking water because you're afraid of drowning. Instead of fearing extreme scenarios, trust your ability to use your gifts responsibly and with loving intention.

Myth: We're not "meant" to explore our intuition.

Truth: Why would we be given abilities if we were not meant to use them? God, or the organizing force of the universe, gave each of us eyes to see with, ears to hear with, hands for touch, a nose for smell, and a mouth for taste. We understand that this natural endowment of physical senses is necessary to navigate our physical reality.

People often don't realize that our visual, auditory, kinesthetic or empathic intuition, mental or cognitive intuition, and olfactory and gustatory intuition are these same physical senses, simply heightened to allow us to perceive spiritual or energetic dimensions.

Why do we have such a hard time seeing these as part of our natural sensory endowment to use freely, comfortably, and effortlessly? They're the same five senses, yet we accept one and fear the other rather than embracing all aspects of them. When we grasp that all of this ability is meant for us to use at different times and for different purposes, then we claim our full human and spiritual inheritance.

Myth: "I can't be intuitive because I don't have the abilities of the psychics like those I see on television."

Truth: Many intuitive people are afraid to explore their abilities because they fear they won't measure up to their notions of what a "real" psychic or medium is or does. These labels conjure up all kinds of images we have seen on TV and in movies, but it never works to assess our lives based on what we see in the media, does it?

Since most of us know so little about intuition, those are often the only examples we have. But as you get to know more intuitive people, you will find there are many forms of intuition—as many different forms as there are people. We are each unique individuals when it comes to intuition, just as with most things.

Think of your own five senses. Your vision may be better or worse than another person. You might have very sensitive hearing or some hearing loss. There are certain smells you love and others you don't. You and I may eat the same food, but it may taste completely differently to each of us. We may both see the same movie, but you may feel very differently about it than I do.

Our intuitive senses work the same way. We will describe the different types of intuition in the next chapter, but the most important thing to know is that no form of intuition is "better" than any other. For example, some energy therapists see energy while others feel the sensations in their own bodies. Still others may receive auditory or cognitive messages. Yes, some can even taste or smell energy!

Our intuition shows up for us in different ways, too. Some people (mediums, for example) naturally connect with those who have passed, while others sense the energy of people around them, including illnesses (medical intuitives), or emotional or spiritual energies. Some people connect with animals or the environment. There are people who can read thoughts, predict weather, or move objects with their minds. All of these gifts appear in varying degrees and combinations, and they can change based on life events or training.

Everyone has some degree of intuitive ability, usually much more than we realize. The question is not if you're an intuitive, because we all are to some degree. Some people's faculties are more heightened, even to the point that these abilities can cause disruption in their lives and their ability to function. I use the example that most everyone can play basketball, but not every player is Michael Jordan. Most people can sense to some degree when someone else is sad. Most people can feel compassion when someone is in pain. But not everyone is intuitively sensitive to the point where they will feel another person's sadness or pain as if it were their own.

On some level, most of us are aware of our abilities, even if we have been doing our best to suppress the knowledge. Often we may have difficulties in our lives that we didn't realize were caused by our inability to integrate our intuitive gifts into our lives. Many times, people slowly begin to recognize that their intuitive abilities have played a large role in their lives since they were children.

This frequently happens with parents of the intuitive children I work with at my center. As their children develop their abilities, the parents recognize their own intuitive gifts that they have ignored, trivialized, or suppressed. The bottom line is that your gifts are unique to you. There is no hierarchy designating some gifts as better than others. While some gifts may be more popular and others may be less discussed or understood, none is more or less valuable than any other.

Myth: Intuition is religious activity.

Truth: Your intuition is no more religious than your sense of sight or smell. It is simply a part of your natural human endowment. Yes, intuition and prophetic knowing has played a significant part in religious tradition, however, so has food and wine, for example, and we don't think of food and wine as religious! Intuition is a normal part of life, and it is neither religious nor anti-religious. Your intuition does not belong to any particular faith any more than your sense of hearing does.

Sometimes someone will tell me that they feel in their heart that I can help them or their children, but they can't see me professionally because "it is against their religion." I don't ever talk anyone into coming to see me, but I think people know in their heart what's true, above and beyond indoctrination.

Sometimes I will ask them, "Do you believe the Bible is the inherent work of God? Do you believe in all of the examples where it is written that, 'the Angel of the Lord appeared to me,' or 'the voice of the Lord spoke to me,' or 'Joseph had a prophetic dream that came true,' or someone laid hands on a person and that person was healed?"

When they say "yes," I ask them if they believe that people stopped having those abilities or gifts after the last book of the Bible was written. Usually they believe there are still people on the planet today who have the ability to see visions, have prophetic dreams, or heal people. I explain that I help these people use and manage their gifts in their daily life.

Sometimes, because people think about intuitive gifts in a biblical or religious context, they believe that intuition can *only* be used in a religious context or by people who are "touched by God."

The truth of the matter is that these gifts are natural extensions of the human senses. They are just the magnified range of the sensory functions given to us to enhance every aspect of our lives. They are not meant to be exclusively bound to a religious or spiritual context, any more than our other senses.

Historically Speaking

Religion has historically been the domain where cultures have stored anything they couldn't explain. Then "it" sits there until there is a scientific or rational explanation for it, and the idea is no longer considered religious. In a short time, that concept moves into the secular and scientific realm of understanding.

For example, at one time we didn't understand what caused rain, so rain dances were performed for the gods so crops would grow. As a scientific understanding of weather patterns emerged, we no longer prayed to the gods for rain. Instead, we looked to meteorology and weather systems to know when to anticipate certain kinds of weather.

The same thing is true for intuitive abilities. Until now, they have been classified as a religious phenomenon or paranormal activity, but they actually are part of our natural human endowment. They are simply a heightened level of the normal senses we use every day (sight, sound, touch, taste, and smell). The conversation around intuition and intuitive abilities became secularized as quantum mechanic theories were discovered in the early twentieth century, and scientists have since then begun to prove the existence of intuitive and psychic abilities.

Intuition and Secular Spirituality

Just because you are intuitive or see or feel energy, doesn't mean you are using those gifts in a religious or even spiritual context. While some people do use their gifts within the context of a specific church or religion, many others do not. If you are able to predict a storm that is coming, or you know your husband is coming down with a cold before he does, there is no religious or spiritual aspect attached to this knowing. You are simply using your sense of intuition.

Intuition is often experienced as part of a larger, nondenominational, philosophical approach that can be described as "secular spirituality." This is becoming more common as people today focus on mutual principles and values that transcend any one religion.

For example, in the Innerlight Method, I use the principles of unity, love, and forgiveness as a foundation for balance and healing.

I believe that our intuition continually draws us back to the source point or unity where we are all one. This oneness can be thought of in many ways: as God, universal consciousness, the superconscious, divine intelligence, One Mind, the Higher Self, or many others. For myself and for many others who develop their intuition, or work with energy, this secular spirituality is not about any particular background or religion.

Instead, we are connecting to the one universal mind, where we can access all that there is to know, all that there has ever been, all that there will ever be, and all range of possibilities. This is not a religious act or experience. Many people and groups evoke their higher source in order to perform secular functions.

For example, a surgeon may pray before entering surgery, but it's not a religious experience when he is performing the surgery. Another example of this is when a football team huddles up before a game to pray for their team to win. Once they get onto the field to play the game, no religion is involved. It's a secular activity. They may call on their own personal spiritual source or team for guidance and support, but the activity they are engaging in is in no way religious.

It is my hope that we can bring an understanding of intuition and energy sensitivity into the mainstream, so that everyone can benefit from the gifts of their intuition, regardless of religious or spiritual background. I believe that by "normalizing" intuition and energy sensitivity—in other words, by taking it out of the "New Age" box, the "psychic" box, or the "spiritual" box—humanity will be able to advance more rapidly, using all of our natural gifts and abilities as they were meant to be used.

For those of you who *are* spiritually (or religiously) inclined, using your intuition can greatly enhance your relationship with the Divine. By squashing and suppressing your gifts, you give away some of your power to contact or co-create with the Divine. You may already be co-creating through techniques such as prayer and meditation. Making yourself more available to intuitive guidance can be another powerful path of spiritual communication.

Because we all have different intuitive gifts, backgrounds, and spiritual beliefs, as well as unique talents and dispositions, we are each able to bring something new and special to the world. When we are able to share from both our intuition and our intellect, we can offer a whole and balanced perspective that fully reflects who we are.

The goal is not for every intuitive person to start a new career as a psychic or get a reality TV show as a medium! While you may want to do that, there are many ways you can contribute to the world, no matter what area of interest or expertise you have. We need intuitive doctors, lawyers, architects, plumbers, and bus drivers too. Imagine how healthy and balanced the world could be if we were all functioning not just from intellect, but from our innermost "higher self" wisdom.

There's only one way to find out what happens next. You have to take a deep breath and leap into the rabbit hole!

Exercises to Face Your Fear

The first step in moving past your fear is to recognize it for the nothingness that it is. Draw a big circle or pie shape and let it represent all your fears about exploring your intuition. Now start naming the "slices." Examples might

be, *"People will think I'm crazy," "I will awaken dark forces,"
"People will think I'm silly," "I will misinterpret a message and
hurt someone," "I will lose credibility at work," "My friends will
avoid me,"* and so forth.

Let these fears simmer for a while and take time to add
other fears as they arise. Once you have all your fears listed,
look at each slice one-by-one. Does it represent something
that has actually happened to you? Or is it just a projection
of what you think "might" happen? What part represents
fear instilled in you by media, stereotypes, books, spiritual
teaching, or your cultural background? If you are like me, or
my students (we often do this exercise as a group), the majority
of your fears are based on projections, not experience.

Journal about each fear, where it came from, and what
you might do to release it.

What helped me most in letting go of my fears was to
start talking to people about my intuition. The more open I
was, the more I realized that many other people are open as
well. I began sharing my intuitive experiences with friends,
family, and co-workers, and found that nine times out of ten
they were not judgmental. In fact, often they happily shared
their own intuitive experiences.

There is one particular instance I fondly recall from the
time when I was anxious to come out of the intuitive closet. I
had recently established a budding friendship with a woman
who invited me to lunch. Before leaving home to meet her,
I decided that if she asked me to talk about what services

I offered in my practice, I would be honest. Sure enough, halfway through lunch she asked me to clarify what I did for a living.

"I'm a psychic and I help energetically sensitive children learn to manage their intuitive abilities," I responded. I don't normally use the word "psychic," but I just didn't want to hedge my answer by saying, "I offer holistic therapy to help children with mood and behavior problems." I couldn't believe those words came out of my mouth! Then I waited for her to get uncomfortable or judge what I had said.

Instead, she started to tell me about how she communicates with the deceased! *What?* I didn't expect that response! I knew she was a successful professional actress, and if I hadn't been honest, she would have never revealed this side of herself. Years later, we now have a deep connection and a lifelong friendship. In fact, because her work as a medium was making her ill, I taught her the Innerlight Method and now she uses it to work with her clients without getting sick.

Don't be fooled by the stories you're telling yourself— that people won't accept who you really are. More and more people are becoming aware of their intuitive abilities and finding ways to integrate them into their daily lives. You may find, as I did, that many of the most intelligent and successful people you know are highly intuitive. Even the people closest to you, your friends and family, may have intuitive experiences and abilities, which you won't find out about unless you start the conversation.

I'm not pretending you won't run into skepticism here and there. I tell my students not to make too much of it or try to convince anyone. There are more than enough people who will understand and honor your intuition. At this point, I'm pretty much immune to any "hecklers." No aspect of my self-esteem is damaged by someone else's judgment or disbelief because I have far too much evidence of the power of intuition.

Every person must come to their own conclusions about how open they want to be. For me, losing a few relationships with closed-minded people is less painful than living an inauthentic, unfulfilled life. The more I learned to accept and manage my gifts, the more amazing people I started to meet. Now my whole life is filled with intuitively gifted people so there is nothing "strange" about me within my community.

We make up the story that we're alone with these abilities. We may even enjoy the idea that we are the "oddball" or the "black sheep" that no one understands. But there is nothing so unusual about you that you need to be sitting in a corner, thinking no one understands what you're going through. There's nothing to be gained by isolating yourself and much to be lost. We don't know how many people are highly intuitive or energetically sensitive, but some estimates are as high as 20-25 percent of the population. That's a significant number of people who can be great resources and offer companionship and inspiration to you!

You can let your fears run the show, but in the end your intuitive gifts are likely to make their presence known in spite of your best efforts to deny them. Trying to bury such an important part of who you are and not learning how to manage it can mean increasing discomfort, depression, anxiety, alienation, illnesses, and a lack of satisfaction with your life and work. You won't feel fully alive, whole, and fulfilled until you allow your complete self to flourish.

As you are journaling about your fears, include the ideas you learned about intuition from your family of origin, school, church, and the media. Also, write about your actual experiences of when you used your intuition and when you didn't. Did you regret using it or not using it? Sit with what bubbles up. Remember that all these memories and ideas are just the beginning of your journey to explore your intuition.

Unmasking the Myths

You are likely to bump up against myths and cultural ideas that make intuition and energy sensitivity seem "wrong." These might include such ideas as:

- It's against God's will to use your intuition or energy sensitivity
- Intuition and energy sensitivity are for hippies only
- Intuitive people are weird or unreliable, spacey, bad with finances, etc.

- Intuitive people are always wearing crystals, big, flowing skirts, and scarves wrapped around their heads, etc.
- To be intuitive, you have to be psychic

There will always be naysayers or people who are afraid of something that is different than what they already know. In order to keep from being swayed by others' uninformed opinions, it's important for you to connect with, and reconcile, your personal beliefs around this work.

Acknowledging what you believe is possible is critically important if you work in a healing field, because your beliefs determine the level of healing your client can tap into on an energetic level. Your limiting personal beliefs are the only thing that will hold you back in developing your intuition. So please take time to explore your personal beliefs surrounding energy and intuition.

Exercise: Release and Replace

Now it's time to eliminate limiting beliefs and replace them with empowering beliefs that will support you moving forward in this work.

Which beliefs or myths above resonated with you? Are there others that you have absorbed from the culture you were raised in that do not support you?

Write out these beliefs on a separate piece of paper. Then rip the piece of paper you wrote your beliefs on into tiny pieces. While tearing the piece of paper, set the intention that you're eliminating and letting go of all beliefs that no longer serve you. Throw it away, flush it down the toilet, or burn it (safely).

Finally, re-write your new beliefs related to your intuition. Write down your new empowering affirmations and beliefs and speak them out loud. Place your new empowering beliefs in a visible area. You want positive reminders as often as possible.

When Fear is Replaced with Truth

Now that you've faced some of your fears around intuition and your own gifts, it's time to get clear about those gifts. In the next chapter, we will explore the six different intuitive pathways and understand more about how intuition expresses itself through you.

2

Step Two: Identify Your Intuitive Gifts

Exploring the Secret Life of the Intuitive

> *"Please tell my mommy to do what the doctor said."*
>
> W*hat?* I looked around me to see where the tiny voice was coming from. I gulped when I saw the pregnant woman standing behind me in the checkout line.
>
> It took me a minute to muster up the courage to reply to the voice through my own thoughts. *I don't want to do this!* I continued placing my items on the counter. I was sure the lady would think I was crazy or be offended if I passed along that message.

This wasn't the first baby to talk to me. I'd heard the voices of several babies in utero, asking me to tell their mommies to eat more vegetables, get more rest, or other random messages that only had meaning to the mother. Again, I thought this was happening because of my own grief from losing Noelle. I'd told my midwife and her colleagues about the pain and voices, and they said they didn't think I was crazy. In fact, they told me that the next time I heard a baby talk to me in a store or park I should share the message with the mom.

So this was it.

When the woman turned to me and smiled, I took that as a cue and plunged ahead. I said, "Hi. I'm learning to work with intuitive energy and sometimes I receive random messages for people."

The woman didn't look offended. Instead, she perked up and said, "Really? I'd love to hear a message."

"I hope you don't think I'm crazy, but I can hear babies talk to me and your baby just asked me to tell you to please do what the doctor said."

The woman stared at me blankly for what felt like an eternity. Just as I started to apologize for bothering her with my message, she began to cry. I stood there stunned while she explained that she was on her way home from a doctor's appointment. There were complications with her pregnancy so her obstetrician recommended special prenatal testing. She had planned to convince her husband that they didn't need the tests, but would now follow the doctor's recommendation. She thanked me for sharing the message as she wiped her tears away.

I said goodbye and turned to finish checking out. My heart began to race with excitement. *Maybe it's not a mental breakdown. Maybe this is a gift that I just have to learn how to use.*

Now that you have faced your fears of being intuitive, it's time to name it and claim it! You are coming out of the intuitive closet, so-to-speak, although it may take some getting used to. For so long, we've hidden our gifts in the dark. We have dreams, feel things, see things, know things—but are careful not to say anything about it, lest anyone think we're silly, strange, delusional, or a know-it-all.

The "secret life" of the intuitive can involve any number of interesting experiences, to say the least. From hearing deceased ancestors, feeling the energy of objects and places, speaking with plants and animals, seeing past lives, or even channeling wisdom from other realms. You may have the ability of astral travel, or the capacity to view experiences far removed from you in distance and/or time. Many people believe that these skills are becoming more commonplace as we open up to new ways of understanding and experiencing consciousness.

There is no limit to the creative uses or value of our intuitive gifts. For example, authors sometimes talk about how their characters came alive and "told them" what to write. Musicians have said that they hear fully composed songs in their head before they start to write. Doctors can use their intuition to help with diagnoses, and scientists can use intuition to make discoveries. Spiritual leaders use their intuition to strengthen their connection to the Divine. We sometimes call these people geniuses, when in truth they have simply given themselves permission to tap into and trust their intuition, and then apply it to their area of passion, talent, and interest.

Why are so many people who create inventions, products, or services from that intuitive place often thought of as unstable or too "out there"? Why are they criticized and ridiculed? Only those who have the persistence to act on it, who come through with breakthroughs, are the winners. They had to fight all of society to be their true self and have learned to set aside convention-based thinking on how they connected, trusted, and acted on their gifts.

You can use your intuition to help you be a better artist, spouse, parent, athlete, employee, or business owner. The possibilities are infinite *if* you're willing to bring your gifts out of the dark.

Am I Intuitive?

"Am I intuitive?" is the number one question I get asked. As I said earlier, since everyone is intuitive, the simple answer is, "Yes, you are!" But not everyone recognizes their own abilities or even wants to recognize them.

What do we mean by the word "intuition?" Intuition is the ability to acquire knowledge without conscious thought or logical processing. When a person operates from intuition, they are certain of clear knowing without being able to explain how they know.

Most people don't recognize that heightened empathic or intuitive faculties are the source of their stress. For example, a couple brought their son to see me. He had been having significant problems adjusting to school life, and had all the classic signs of empathic overload. After one Innerlight Method session with me things changed dramatically. He was able to have play dates and eat in the school cafeteria. His parents said it was like having their son back. Then they brought their daughter to see me and the scenario was the same. She was highly empathic and it was causing anxiety for her, and the energy balancing therapy helped her tremendously.

The mother had no problem recognizing that her children were intuitive, yet when she described difficulties she had in her own life and I suggested that she was experiencing intuitive overload as well, she said, "Oh no, not me! There's nothing intuitive about me." In my experience with thousands of families, if the children are intuitive, the parents are too. But so often, as adults, we don't see it.

There appears to be a significant acceleration of intuition and sensitivity with each generation, so the intuitive overload can be stronger for children. This only adds to the intuitive overload the parents may already be feeling. It's easy to see how intuitive families can become overwhelmed and feel out of control.

Research shows that our brains are wired to be intuitive from the moment we are born. It's only a question of how much we have filtered out of our intuitive abilities over the years. Often we learn to block them during childhood. Think of our aptitude to learn languages. We're born with a high capability to learn many languages, but as we listen to just one, our brains start to selectively narrow and focus our attention on that specific dialect. The same is true with our intuitive abilities. We start out with an ability to learn multi-dimensionally, but then we're trained in what we should see, hear, and feel—and what we should *not* see, *not* hear, and *not* feel.

We're acculturated to select for the logical or the "known," and soon we become blinded to other perceptions. Remember the story of Columbus coming to America and the Native Americans not being able to see the boats because they didn't know what they were—there was no such thing in their frame of reality, so they simply could not "see" the boats. There is a whole dimension (many dimensions, really) of energy and experience around us that we all have the ability to perceive once we give ourselves permission to look.

The Six Intuitive Pathways

Just as with any other faculty, everyone's natural intuitive abilities are different. You can think of intuition as an umbrella term that covers many traits and abilities.

The invitation is always there for every person to tap into this ability. How each of us is able to access the energy fields around us depends on the senses we engage the most. Our five senses allow us to perceive the three-dimensional world, but they can also help us perceive beyond that.

Our dominant senses and learning styles will help us the most in our quest to understand our intuition. I have found in my practice that most people's intuitive abilities typically correlate with their learning styles. If you're a visual learner, you're more likely to be a visual intuitive or clairvoyant and have the ability to see beyond what the average human eye sees. Auditory learners may be able to hear voices or thoughts. For example, Luther Burbank, an American botanist, horticulturist, and pioneer in agricultural science, famously said his plants spoke to him.

Kinesthetic learners, who learn by doing, often are clairsentient and feel others' energy and emotions in their own bodies. Mental intuitives access the world of energy through claircognizance, or a sense of knowing. They might know the answer to a complex math equation without even knowing how they know.

Then there is clairgustance, or the ability to get energetic information through the sensation of taste, and clairolfaction, or sensing energy through smell. For example, I could tell my father was sick when I repeatedly smelled his cologne, even though he was not nearby. You may smell fire and then realize you left your stove on. In that case, your olfactory intuition could save your life! The good news is that we can learn to balance, regulate, and apply our intuition to greatly enhance our life experience. We all have tremendous potential to expand and develop our intuitive abilities.

Every human being has access to all six intuitive pathways; however, not all are equally developed. By becoming conscious of one's primary intuitive pathway, a person can begin to intentionally use their intuitive gifts to activate their genius potential. The six intuitive pathways are: visual, auditory, mental, kinesthetic, gustatory, and olfactory.

#1- Visual Intuitives

Visual intuitives process subconscious guidance through their external or internal sight. Insights appear to them as pictures, movies, or images that flash before their eyes. They are able to see energy fields, auras, or spirits that are not perceptible to others. Visual intuitives think in symbols and often receive guidance through vivid dreams.

#2- *Auditory Intuitives*

Auditory intuitives process subconscious guidance through sound. They have the ability to hear lyrics to new songs or musical notes. Like Charles Dickens, they can hear stories or entire novels being dictated to them in their minds. Some auditory intuitives are so sensitive that they can actually hear other people's thoughts. Great speakers are usually gifted with auditory intuition. Many describe this ability as having "a voice in my head that tells me how to say or do things in the best possible way."

#3- *Mental Intuitives*

Mental (or cognitive) intuitives have the enhanced ability to process sudden flashes of understanding that lead to new theories or solutions to problems. Their subconscious guidance quickly combines separate pieces of disconnected information and reorganizes them into a coherent whole. Mental intuitives shine when they access instant illumination that leads to new inventions.

#4- *Kinesthetic Intuitives*

Kinesthetic (or empathic) intuitives engage through heightened body awareness. They have an enhanced ability to subconsciously register and react to feelings, taste, touch, or smell. They sense the energy in their environment and are affected by it more directly than others. Kinesthetic intuitives operate from "gut instinct" and access knowing through their physical response to their environment. They know when things don't "feel right" to them.

Unfortunately, many kinesthetic intuitives actually take on and embody other people's emotions, illnesses, pains, and energy. This can lead them to avoid social situations or experience extreme social anxiety in unfamiliar or uncomfortable places. Healers, teachers, ministers, therapists, or others in helping professions are often what is called an intuitive empath or kinesthetic intuitive. Because they are unaware of their intuitive profile, they experience high rates of burnout and fatigue from taking on their clients' or students' energy.

#5- Gustatory Intuitives

Gustatory intuitives have the enhanced ability to pick up intuitive information through their sense of taste. For example, I know a holistic healer who gets a distinct taste of metal in her mouth whenever she is working with clients who have heavy metal toxicity. Whenever she experiences this specific flavor when working with a client, she intuitively knows she needs to conduct further testing to see which heavy metal the client needs to clear from their body. Gustatory intuitives make genius level chefs who can "just taste" what makes a dish come alive.

#6- *Olfactory Intuitives*

Olfactory intuitives have the enhanced ability to process intuitive information through their sense of smell. For example, they may smell the scent of a specific perfume when no one is physically around them. However, if this scent was worn by a familiar person, the scent may trigger a connection with that person and can sometimes be a means of transmitting an intuitive message. While less common than the other faculties, olfactory intuition is just as valuable when processing information that your client is trying to communicate to you. Olfactory intuitives make great perfumers or aromatherapy practitioners.

As you read this, you might find that you have more than one of these gifts, as do I. Usually, we find that we are stronger in some areas of intuition and weaker in others. The important thing is to get a sense of where you are on the spectrum so you can choose to develop your gifts and find your unique genius.

I am a multisensory intuitive. When my gifts first opened up, I primarily experienced intuitive connection by literally feeling it in my body. This is empathic or kinesthetic intuition, when information comes through signals and feelings in the body. How does that differ from instinct? I make the distinction between survival instincts, which send me danger alerts to keep me safe, and kinesthetic intuition, which provides useful guidance and information for me or for others. For example, if I get chills or my stomach churns when I am in a situation that could be harmful to me, that is gut instinct. If I feel a sensation or pain that is connected to a message for someone, I know I am being guided in that moment to help another person.

I also hear messages. Auditory intuition for me sounds like I'm having a conversation and I hear it as clearly as I hear "normal" conversations.

I don't have a particularly strong olfactory or gustatory intuition, and I do not see energy around people with my eyes open as some visual intuitives do. But with my inner intuitive sight (my eyes closed), I see images of what needs to be addressed in the person I am working with at that moment.

When I was a child, I didn't have to work hard to do well in school. I could hear a voice that told me the right answers. My approach to learning was an intuitive process, although I didn't know it at the time. Cognitive or mental intuition comes to me as completely formed knowing, beyond anything I could know any other way. I experience it as knowledge that just lands like a butterfly on my shoulder. It is exciting! When knowledge comes through to me like this, it's so clear that it is better than anything I could have thought of myself.

Sometimes mental intuition works for me as a kind of funnel that blends information from many sources to create something special. Through cognitive intuition, I can see connections between a wide variety of ideas and concepts, and am able to synthesize them into new developments and programs. That's how I created the Innerlight Method.

Your intuitive gifts are likely to be a combination like mine. Your intuitive pathways are trying to connect with you and get your attention. When you put them together into the supercomputer of your mind, the result can be significant insights and breakthroughs that defy logic, and can take your work and life in bold new directions.

Recognizing the Intuitive Child

While this book is not primarily about children (that is the subject of a forthcoming book), I wanted to talk a little about the intuitive child for two reasons: to help you better understand the children in your life and perhaps to give you insights into your own childhood.

Often when I talk about the experiences of my child clients who are intuitive, my adult clients will say, "Where were you when I was a child? I had similar experiences when I was young, but I had no way to understand what was happening."

While most children have access to the basic five senses, children who are perceived as intuitive, or energetically sensitive, experience one or more of their senses at a heightened or amplified level. Often these children have sensory capabilities that are far beyond the average child. For example, a visually sensitive child may see auras of color, or even beings that others do not see. A child with auditory sensitivity may hear sounds at two or three times the decibel level of most children.

These heightened sensitivities can create challenges for the energetically sensitive child and for their families. A child with a heightened sense of hearing may not be able to function well in loud environments that are appealing to many other children, such as being in a Chuck E. Cheese's restaurant. Energetically sensitive children often complain about the way their clothes touch them, such as labels, tags, or seams in socks. Some energetically sensitive children can't stand to wear socks or closed-toe shoes and would rather go barefoot, even in the wintertime.

A child with a heightened sense of smell may be bothered by the slightest odor. They may only be able to eat bland food and could have a complete meltdown when sitting at a table with multiple types of food because the strong, competing smells are too much for them.

Empaths, or emotionally sensitive children, often have meltdowns in crowds or crowded rooms. Sometimes they can only manage five or six people in a room at a time, because they are feeling the emotions and pains of the people around them. Empathic children may not want to go to Disneyland, or they might hide in a room or a closet when the family invites guests over. Some of them are auditory empaths and can hear what other people are thinking. They can pick up on the emotional energetics of classmates as well as teachers, and may act out with aggression or express a behavior of being in "overwhelm."

Energetically sensitive children typically have a combination of sensitivities, with one area in particular causing the most difficulty. The energetically sensitive child may be defiant or withdrawn at home or in school, and may have tantrums or seem rude because they don't want to hug someone or be close to others.

Unfortunately, these children can be labeled as antisocial, poorly behaved, or worse. People might see them as whiny, or think they just need to "grow up" or "suck it up." But imagine what it must be like to live with such heightened sensitivity. For an average adult, it would be like being locked in a crowded arena with a heavy metal concert that never ends!

Relief is possible. I use the Innerlight Method to help clients bring the nervous system into balance, and educate parents and children about tools and strategies to manage their sensitivities. After energy balancing, I have seen countless children dramatically improve their ability to function at home, in school, and out in the world. Instead of blaming parents or teachers, or referring a child for disciplinary action or medication, we need to address energetic sensitivities as a first step. There is hope and help available for energetically sensitive children and their families.

Once you become more aware of how the child's gifts present themselves, you can work with the child so that they can consciously use them as a resource rather than a hindrance. If you think of life as a game of consciousness (and in so many ways, it is), why not choose to play the game with every strategy available to you?

Intuition is Not a Crystal Ball

Now, just a few words on what being an intuitive is *not*. Being intuitive doesn't make life problem-free for any of us. As far as I know, no one has perfect intuition, and even the most intuitive people have challenges. We have limits and weaknesses, and we make mistakes. None of that negates our intuitive ability. We are still human!

Being an intuitive doesn't wash away every experience of pain, but it does let us walk through life with a greater sense of comfort, awareness, and guidance. It can help us get more quickly and directly to what is in the highest and best interest for us, and give us a broader understanding when things don't work out that something even greater is being lined up.

While we may have advance knowledge of some things, or be able to improve our lives in many ways because of our intuition, not everything will turn out the way we want. Sometimes we don't want to end up with what we think we want. In fact, it's better that we don't! Even the times when intuition tells us no, it can help us be more at peace with what's unfolding in our life.

Many of us want to win the lottery, stop another World War, and make the person of our dreams bow down at our feet and never leave us. But what would life be if it were laid out every day exactly as we asked for it?

Even when life doesn't match our expectations, our intuition can give us insight into what is unfolding, so that we can act with peace and grace. For example, when a close friend received a medical diagnosis, I knew immediately that she was going to die. This is not what I wanted at all, and I certainly didn't share that knowledge with her, but it did help prepare me for what was coming.

If I could have changed the death of my baby, I would have, but intuition did not help me with that. It only gave me a forewarning of what was to come in a way that somewhat softened the blow. Intuition is not always about making us happy or directing outcomes. Instead, it helps us surrender to the greater flow of the universe and to our larger place within the dance of this life.

Illness and death can be particularly difficult challenges. That is only because many of us have been conditioned to narrow our focus, desires, and aspirations to consider only our immediate senses on this plane. Our souls did not enter our bodies to be contained forever. Although greater freedom may lie beyond this life, we have been conditioned to believe this physical experience is "everything." Intuition can give us the big picture and remind us what our soul came here to do and be. It can help us remember that this is just a pit stop on our larger soul journey, and align us with the bigger vision of why we exist that goes beyond our conditioning. This can be an especially important perspective for intuitives who work in healing fields. Our goal is not to use our intuitive knowing or healing ability to keep every person alive! Eventually, every soul needs a reason to exit the body.

Intuition gives us more comfort in knowing that in each situation we will be given the guidance we need, whether the situation is something we perceive as positive or negative. Through intuition, we can often access insight and foresight to accept the journey as it is unfolding with more grace, relief, and inner peace.

When we acknowledge and claim our intuition, we are truly accepting our gifts in surrender to the larger flow of the universe. We are recognizing our place in the dance of life. As intuition helps us to navigate our focus, desires, and aspirations, it can guide us to our true purpose in life. Intuition can help us break free from our "domestication" as author Don Miguel Ruiz says, so that we can step into a larger sense of universal possibility.

When you say yes to your intuition, it's a little like standing in line for the Space Mountain ride at Disneyland. You don't know exactly what you're in for because it's dark. You don't know where the dips and inclines are going to be, but you have to trust in the safety of the experience and enjoy the ride. You need to surrender to the process and trust where it is leading you.

Exercise: Identify Your Intuitive Gifts

Below is just a sample of characteristics (not a complete list) of the different types of intuitives. Intuition is a highly individual experience. What do you *think* is your primary intuitive pathway? Do you have more than one? Why do you believe this to be true? (Hint: Chances are you're connected to your intuition on at least one level already!) Remember that no intuitive pathway is better than any other. Your intuitive gifts are as unique as you are.

Type 1: Energetically Sensitive Kinesthetic Intuitive
- Seems to absorb the emotions or physical symptoms of others
- Can sense even the smallest energetic shifts in their environment
- Actively avoids large crowds
- Has extreme anxiety not related to trauma

Type 2: Energetically Sensitive Visual Intuitive
- Sees deceased loved ones, spirits
- Sees auras and colors around people
- Has vivid dreams and/or dreams that come true

- Can determine a person's well-being by visualizing their energy field
- Sees images of past or future events
- Sees images or pictures in the environment around them that others do not see

Type 3: Energetically Sensitive Auditory Intuitive

- Hears and channels music, speeches, or written work
- Hears inner voices that give reliable guidance and support
- Experiences telepathy or the ability to hear others' thoughts
- Has a heightened sense of hearing
- Experiences the world around them through sound and music

Type 4: Energetically Sensitive Mental Intuitive

- Has frequent flashes of knowing
- Can solve complex math problems without writing out the work
- Takes seemingly disconnected information and synthesizes it to come up with an invention or theory that seems unconnected to the parts, but is a new high-level concept
- Experiences frequent, unexplained headaches
- Has sleep problems
- Can't stop thinking

Type 5: Energetically Sensitive Gustatory Intuitive

- Receives intuitive messages by tasting substances that are not actually in their mouth at the time
- Can't handle different tastes and textures of food in their mouths
- Very picky eaters
- Doesn't like different foods to touch each other on their plate
- Likes to eat one type of food at a time

Type 6: Energetically Sensitive Olfactory Intuitive

- Receives intuitive messages by smelling things that are not physically present
- Is super-sensitive to smell
- Avoids perfume departments and stores that smell
- Is more sensitive to synthetic chemicals and other household cleaners
- Ends up being a picky eater because they're overwhelmed by the smells of specific food.

Now that you know what your primary intuitive pathway is, I encourage you to go out into the world and start noticing how it has always been "trying" to lead you on a daily basis.

Every time you notice your intuition communicating with you, stop and pause to acknowledge it. Note whether your intuition is coming to you as an image, a sound or conversation, a feeling, a thought or idea, a taste or a smell. Remember that we can often develop the styles that are weaker by paying attention and applying intention.

Journal and record what you notice on a daily basis. How does your life shift when you lean into and trust your intuition? (*Note*: The act of writing and journaling is proven to help connect people to their intuitive senses.)

Time to Own It

Now that you've identified your intuitive gift(s), it's time to look at some of the challenges that people with similar gifts often face and learn how to mitigate them.

3

Step Three:
Claim Your Power

Overcoming the Healer's Dilemma

Standing on stage, I could feel it starting to happen. It literally felt like every beautiful soul in the audience "hooked up" to me (energetically) the minute I stood behind the podium.

Niki, come on. Plug into your spiritual support. You've got this. You have more than enough energy. Let Spirit work through you. It's your ministry to share this message with the people in front of you.

After giving myself this brief pep talk, I opened my mouth and let Spirit speak through me. It was a powerful session, and I could feel the elevation of every person in the room.

Feeling a bit high from the energy coursing through me, I walked off the stage into a throng of people, many of whom held their hands out to me. I shook hands as I made my way to the back of the room, noticing that the "high" I was feeling was being replaced by something else. *What is happening to me?* It had happened several times before and I knew what was coming.

I finally reached my car and drove about a mile down the road before I had to pull over to throw up. *Why does this keep happening?* I asked, as I wiped my face and sat back in the car. *I am wiped out. I feel like I've been drained of every ounce of energy. Maybe some lunch will help...*

On the way home I grabbed some dark chocolate and a cup of coffee, just to help pick me up while I made my lunch. I felt a little better immediately, but the exhaustion wouldn't go away.

I guess I'm going to spend the rest of the day in bed, the way I did last week. After eating, I took a shower, put on my pajamas, and did nothing but lay in bed for the rest of the day.

Although we all see, hear, touch, taste, and smell, intuitive or energetically sensitive individuals have senses that function beyond the range of the average person. We all have the capacity for tapping into our intuitive faculties, but for people who are overly sensitive, their awareness is so heightened that can prohibit them from being able to function optimally in normal daily life. This can give the appearance of learning, mood, attention, and behavioral challenges, among other things.

People with heightened intuitive faculties and senses may have difficulty concentrating. These problems are sometimes misinterpreted as ADHD or other learning, mood, or behavior challenges. The amount of stimuli coming into a sensitive person's nervous system may cause an internal experience of feeling like they're stuck with a drum pounding inside their head all day long. With this much stimuli coming in, it is easy to understand why they cannot function normally in a classroom or work environment.

Intuitive people often hold pain that doesn't belong to them without realizing it. Problems can include back and knee pain, depression, anxiety, and much more. When my own intuition opened up and I began feeling pain, disease, and the emotional states of others, I was unable to distinguish it from my own experience. I went to doctor after doctor with my complaints—headaches, stomach aches, and all kinds of pains—but they said there was nothing wrong with me, and implied that I was a hypochondriac!

This is the healer's dilemma: we are given gifts that can help or even heal others and ourselves, but they can also hurt us if we don't know how to manage our abilities. Culturally, we have a romanticized view of intuitive abilities. We think people with psychic or intuitive abilities are special and lucky to be so gifted. But that isn't always how it feels to be an intuitive, especially when we develop illnesses or "burnout" due to our inability to regulate the energies we are taking into our energy field.

For many people, it can feel more like a curse than a blessing when you can't stay at a party for more than twenty minutes, you become overloaded at a work function, or you become so exhausted and burned out that you have to leave your chosen career altogether. We usually learn to hide or suppress our intuitive gifts at a fairly young age and this adds to our physical or emotional challenges.

Intuitives often question their mental health and become increasingly introverted, reclusive, or even agoraphobic. Parents of intuitive children struggle with how to explain what's happening to their children, and ask me, "Can you explain to my child why his abilities are an asset and not a liability?"

Here are some of the challenges that intuitive people experience:

- Struggle with behavior, attention, mood, or learning challenges
- Seem anxious, withdrawn, or depressed
- Suffer from frequent stomach pains or digestive problems
- Are energetically sensitive to sounds, light, and colors
- Tend to avoid crowded places like Disneyland or concert venues
- Constantly daydream or seem to live in a fantasy world
- Are exceptionally affected by other people's emotions or moods
- Have unexplained temper tantrums or anger outbursts
- Experience night terrors or fear sleeping in their bedroom
- Exhibit anxiety behaviors such as head banging, nail biting, cutting, or teeth grinding
- Numb themselves with addictive or compulsive behaviors
- Easily experience sensory overload
- Have difficulty aligning with the world around them
- Have frequent feelings of disorientation

Numbing the Sensitivity

Many intuitives have been told they are "too sensitive," either as children or adults. It is fundamentally true—you are more sensitive than many people, but that isn't a bad thing! Unfortunately, because intuitive people often believe there might be something "wrong" with them, and they don't know how to handle the sensory overload, they can look for ways to numb their sensitivity.

Self-numbing behaviors can include withdrawing socially, using legal or illegal drugs, overeating, or any number of other addictions. With intuitive children, we see anxiety behaviors that are either explosive or implosive.

Children's *explosive* behaviors are a more aggressive release of pent-up energy, such as bolting from the room, hitting themselves or others, or throwing chairs or other items. These behaviors are more often associated with boys, and tend to get more immediate intervention because their ways of clearing overloaded energy are more dangerous to the environment.

Implosive releases of energy are more self-injurious, more associated with girls, and less likely to glean attention. They can include cutting behavior, plucking eyelashes, pulling hair, grinding teeth, biting skin, and overeating to build a buffer between themselves and others.

While these behaviors can indeed release energy and numb sensitivity, at least for a time, they also create additional problems and contribute to a vicious cycle of discomfort and dissatisfaction that can continue into adulthood.

The Over-Stressed Nervous System

We process sensory information through our nervous system, the network that transmits nerve impulses throughout the body. The whole point of the nervous system is to receive, interpret, and respond to stimuli, including intuitive stimuli.

When we pick up intuitive information from our environment, it comes to us initially through our energy field and our chakra system. The sensory information then enters our physical being through our solar plexus or stomach area, and travels through our nervous system to whichever intuitive faculty is the strongest. If you are an auditory intuitive, the intuitive information you have picked up comes through your energy field, your chakras, your solar plexus, and travels through your nervous system to your ears where it translates that energy into audible voice or sound that you can hear as intuitive information.

If you are a visual intuitive, the same information would come through your energy field, your chakras, endocrine glands, solar plexus, and your nervous system to travel to your eyes and give you an image of that information. Each person will receive the information differently, even through several intuitive faculties. For a kinesthetic intuitive or empath, that information stays in the solar plexus or stomach area and creates a feeling or a body sensation, which is why empathic people have problems with stomach aches and digestive issues. When the nervous system is overloaded, their intuitive information can accumulate and stay in the stomach area creating havoc with their body.

Unless you learn to manage the intuitive information you pick up, you will feel constantly bombarded. Your nervous system becomes chronically overworked and stressed because you never get a chance to switch from the sympathetic to the parasympathetic nervous system. You are constantly scanning, picking up, and receiving intuitive information from the environment, and your nervous system never gets a chance to calm down.

This is the situation many intuitive adults and children find themselves in, particularly as more people become conscious of their abilities to sense information beyond what is typically believed to be available through our five senses. I believe, as many do, that we are currently in an age where more people than ever before are waking up to these abilities.

It is certainly the case in education where we see more children than ever before exhibiting both intuitive capabilities and the anxious behaviors that go along with them. While there is a tendency to label and medicate these children (as there is with adults), I have found that helping people manage their sensory overload can be a much more effective solution. This method enhances their vast intuitive potential rather than quashing it.

I see so many children and adults who are highly sensitive and intuitive and have mood, anxiety, and nervous conditions, stomach-related issues, or other physical ailments. The best response to the "healer's dilemma" is to learn to turn down the volume on that steady influx of intuitive information that we are constantly scanning and processing from our environment.

Most people don't know how to turn down the volume or "empty the energy trash can" that keeps filling up as they absorb someone else's pain, pick up information from dreams that keep them up at night, see visions, or hear voices, etc. Think of your intuitive trash can as being similar to the one on your computer. It fills up with intuitive "data" until you're drowning in intuitive overload, which then expresses itself through explosive or implosive behaviors.

You become irritable, sabotage your health with compulsive behaviors, or withdraw from social engagements. The problem is that you haven't been able to control the rate of information coming in to you. It's like not building a dam to control a raging river. You find yourself drowning because you didn't have the proper mechanisms to prevent the flood from happening in the first place.

Learning to Talk Back

Most people think that because they're intuitive, it's their destiny (or curse) to take in everything that comes to them. Some people may think, "After all, isn't that why the gift is there? Do I have any choice but to experience it as it comes to me?"

But that *is not* how we use our usual five senses! For example, when there is a boom box playing music too loudly, you don't say, "Well, because I have ears to hear, I have to listen to this at a level 10." If someone is blasting loud music that's giving you a headache, you don't say, "I have to listen because I have ears to hear." No, you say, "Turn that music down!" If bright strobe lights are making you crazy, you don't say, "I have to stay here because I have eyes to see, even though it's making me feel crazy." You leave or you say, "Turn the lights off!"

We regulate our physical senses, so why do we feel we can't regulate our intuitive senses? We have intuitive eyes to see, intuitive ears to hear, kinesthetic intuition that we feel in our body, but we don't think to say, "How do I turn this off, or turn it down?" Or we *do* try to turn it down, consciously or unconsciously, with harmful, numbing behaviors.

The truth is that you have to regulate your intuitive senses just as you do your other senses, so you can engage with them at a volume or at a level that feels comfortable for you at the time. We just haven't been taught how to do this!

As an educator and an energy therapist, I have seen the huge difference it makes when children and adults learn to regulate their intuitive information flow. When highly sensitive people have the appearance of behavior and mood disorders, learning to manage their intuition or energetic sensitivity has solved the problem much of the time. Often it was an energy problem and not a mental health problem at all. In some cases, it is a combination of both that can be helped by energy balancing *and* mental health intervention. I have seen a significant reduction or even complete elimination of behavior, mood, or physical conditions when a person is taught how to manage their intuitive faculties.

The most important message I can share with you to resolve the healer's dilemma is that you're not meant to take your gifts just in the way they come to you. You don't have to accept being overwhelmed by them all the time. You're not supposed to say, "Well, everywhere I go, I hear what's going on with people, or I feel what's happening to them." What that really means is you don't have healthy energy boundaries! You're supposed to be able to open and close the intuitive door at the appropriate times, for the sake of your own health and happiness, as well as the health and happiness of others.

That was absolutely the most liberating discovery for me on my journey as a highly sensitive intuitive. As I said, at one point, I begged for my gifts to go away and I even stopped using them for almost four years because I was so overwhelmed with intuitive information. I thought I had to see everything, hear everything, and feel everything that came to me, so, of course, I became overloaded. The turning point for me was when I learned I could regulate what was happening. That was when I became able to truly integrate my gifts into my life and work.

Sometimes intuitive people put a high value on what they *can't* do. For example, "I can't hold a job because I'm too sensitive. I can't spend too much time with my family. I can't work with computers because of my electromagnetic frequencies," and so forth. While it is true that sensitivity can create challenges, it is absolutely *not* true that you have to be a victim of your sensitivity. I don't believe the divine plan is for anyone to live a limited life because they're intuitive. When people become overly attached to their identity as a "sensitive" person, I sometimes say, "You're not that special! Learn to turn that stuff off so you can get out and live your life!" We are all meant to live in harmony, self-authority, inner peace, and freedom. I believe it's our spiritual inheritance.

By regulating my intuitive information intake, I am able to be at peace with my gifts and use them to their fullest. Do I have 100 percent perfect control? Of course not. Life doesn't work that way. For example, as an empath, am I ever going to be able to enjoy a long vacation in Las Vegas? Probably not, but I can enjoy it for a day despite all the sights, sounds, crowds, and hyper-stimulation. I just know my limits and how long I can stay in a specific environment before I have to take some time out. In fact, my extended family loves to celebrate birthdays, holidays, and special occasions in Las Vegas. Consequently, I've learned how to take care of myself in that environment so I can participate and celebrate with loved ones.

Will I ever choose Las Vegas as a place to go for my energetic restoration, healing, and joy? Never! But that doesn't mean my life is cut off from it. Do I like to go into the noisy environment of Chuck E. Cheese's? Of course not! But can I survive it long enough to enjoy a child's birthday party? Absolutely.

I work with so many families where one person doesn't have the tools to manage their experience, and as a result, the whole family dynamic is upset. For example, the family goes on vacation to Disneyland and everyone has to go home because of one person's meltdown. Of course, they're all angry with the sensitive person who can't handle the environment, but it doesn't have to be that way. I work with children all the time (and adults, too), who learn how to dial down their intuition so they can spend the day at Disneyland or a similar place without incident.

People also sometimes feel that if they "shut it off" they might lose their gift, similar to the way a beginning artist might feel that if they miss an inspiring moment, they will never experience another one. But artists learn that in order to actually produce art and also perfect their craft, they can't afford to rely on inspiration alone. They trust that as they develop their talents, more stimulation will come. In the same way, you will find that as you practice regulating your intuition, your gifts will grow and become more useful.

When your intuitive abilities are calibrated to a level that is best for you at the present time, you can experience energetic balance and function normally and optimally throughout your day.

Exercises: Claim Your Power

In this section, I'm going to share some strategies to help you exercise more power or authority over your gifts instead of fearing them. You can learn to regulate them rather than run from them. The goal is to have a proactive, empowered relationship with your intuitive faculties. You're meant to control them. They are not meant to run or ruin your life.

Keep in mind that intuitive teachers or energy therapists can help you greatly with learning to regulate your gifts, as we will discuss in chapter four. The Innerlight Method I teach can be done in person or remotely, and is designed specifically to help intuitive people learn to regulate and balance their energy sensitivities. The skills and tools I'm sharing here are the same skills I use regularly to manage my own intuitive experience, so they are powerful enough to do the same for you. However, I know that some people will practice them and yet not experience sufficient relief until they work with an energy therapist and release the energetic overload that has compromised their system. (For more information, see "About the Innerlight Method" sessions in the back of the book.) I recommend you begin with the exercises offered in this book and see how far you can get on your own. You may even want to keep a journal to record your experiences and progress.

Use Your Intention

We can think of intuition as a "game" of consciousness. There's much we don't understand yet about consciousness, but looking at it as a game can help us see the possibilities and also not take things too seriously. Play is an important part of how consciousness, genius, and intuition work.

We do know that attention and intention play a powerful role in consciousness, and they are what drive and regulate intuitive gifts. That's why just becoming aware that you have the ability to regulate your gifts can create powerful changes. You can control your intuition and energetic sensitivities internally, from within the self, and with conscious attention and intention. It sounds simple (and many aspects of working with consciousness are simpler than we might imagine), but it takes practice. Often, finding a teacher or group to work with can be helpful as well.

Your first step is to set the rules with clear intention. Everyone has different rules that work for their game. For example, I set an intention that when I step out of my office building and go to pick up my children from school, or I'm in line at a grocery store, or having fun with my children, I don't want to feel anything that goes on with anybody! I am off duty! The only information I want to slip through that intention gate are intuitive hits regarding true and present danger alerts. If it's not a survival alert, I don't want to feel Suzy Q's knee pain behind me in line at the store, or know what my Uber driver is feeling about the argument she had last night with her boyfriend. I'm not interested. I'm closed for business!

But when I invite you into my office because we have a scheduled appointment and you have given me permission, or we have made an agreement to work together energetically, then I set my intention to "yes" and I dial my gifts up to the highest possible level so all my intuitive faculties can be actively engaged to support your healing goals. Once the session is done, I use my intention to shut off that faculty and I'm done for the time being. Our gifts should not be "turned on" 24 hours a day, 7 days a week. That's like leaving your front door wide open with no screen and wondering why you have an animal safari trekking through your house!

Setting your intention can be as simple as setting times that work for you, and saying to yourself, "Now I'm ready. My channels are open to receive. Please send me the download." Or, when you are finished, say to yourself, "I'm turned off now. Can I please not hear voices while I'm on my romantic date this afternoon?" Or, "I set my intention to have a good night's sleep tonight without interruption."

If you choose, you can select certain words or phrases, breathing exercises, meditations, or visualizations to accompany or reinforce your intention. Various intuitive, psychic, or healing methods and teachers have their own routines or rituals, and you may want to experiment to find what works for you. The important thing is to set the clear intention to take charge of your intuitive experiences.

Negotiate Intuitive Deals!

I had to learn that I didn't have to say yes to every gift, just because I had it! We can negotiate with the universe. For example, some intuitive people set an intention like this: "I am happy to hear intuitive messages, but I'd rather not know when someone is going die." Another example: "I'm willing to see someone's guardian angel, but I don't want to see all of their relatives who have passed." When I conduct energy balancing sessions, I ask that relatives who have passed speak through one voice to simplify and minimize confusion.

The point I'm trying to make is that you can prune your intuitive gifts to develop what feels comfortable, and say no to what doesn't feel right. In this way, you don't have to shut down or numb yourself to all your intuitive faculties. You can choose the ones you feel drawn to or that can help you with your goals (the ones that will give you more access to your unique genius potential), and refuse the ones that are not helpful or useful to you. Don't worry. Should you want to re-gain access to any of your gifts later, you can do so easily. These are not permanent choices. In fact, you can make them on a daily basis, depending on your circumstances.

The Intuition Dial Exercise

This exercise was inspired by the work of Ron Davis, author of *The Gift of Learning*. He developed an energy dial exercise to help children with dyslexia and ADHD learn to regulate their physical energy. After seeing how it helped my daughter improve her focus, I decided to adapt the exercise to help intuitive people regulate the use of their gifts.

The Intuition Dial Exercise can help you learn how to use intention to manage sensory input and overload. Begin by drawing your energy and awareness to your solar plexus, and breathe deeply several times. Take the palm of your hand and hold it a few inches in front of your navel to focus your attention on this area, to represent your kinesthetic intuition.

Now ask, "At what level, on a scale from zero to ten, is my kinesthetic or empathic intuition right now?" Zero is the level where you are completely shut off from all information. At this level, you are probably completely unconscious! Ten is the level where you are completely open to 100 percent access capacity. Now listen for the answer, which may come as a sound, a thought, a feeling, an image, or an idea. Don't worry about thinking you are imagining it. Just go with whatever comes.

Let's say you get the feeling of a nine. Now ask another question, "What level is optimal for me at this time?" Let's say you get the feeling of a three. So to close the gap between nine and three, visualize turning down the volume of that faculty using a motion with your hand as if you were turning down the volume of a radio or closing a jar, with a "righty-tighty" clockwise turn.

Feel, see, or imagine yourself turning it down from nine to eight to seven to six to five to four to three. There! Now you are at the correct level of kinesthetic intuition for your present circumstances. Remember you can change it or dial it back up at any time using this exercise (particularly helpful for beginners), or simply through intention.

Now do the same visualization and motion for each of your faculties, starting with your palm in front of your eyes for visual intuition, beside one of your ears for auditory intuition, above the crown of your head for cognitive or mental intuition, in front of your mouth for gustatory intuition, and in front of your nose for olfactory intuition. One-by-one, re-set your receptivity of each gift to the level that is appropriate for you and feel the shift.

At any time when you feel you want to shift your receptivity up or down, or even just check in with where you are, you can do this exercise. One of the biggest challenges is to recognize when you need to dial up or down, because you are probably used to ignoring or suppressing this particular gift. For example, you may be studying and want to dial your intuition up to help your learning process. You may want to dial up your intuition when you are working with a client, teaching a class, engaging in artistic efforts, or seeking spiritual guidance.

Just remember to turn it back down! You may want to dial down your senses, for example, to make your sense of taste or smell less acute when you are in close quarters with other people and food is present. You may want to dial down your receptivity at night before you go to bed so you can rest more deeply.

It is never a static or permanent adjustment. You are in control and can determine what is optimal for you at any time. The more you practice, the more quickly you will be able to dial your faculties up and down.

Your Secret Weapon: Grounding

One of the most important "secrets" for intuitives to understand is the importance of grounding. Because intuitive people spend so much time in right-brain experience, aware of the more abstract or larger aspects of the human experience such as spiritual connection, energy sensitivity, or intuitive messages, they can find it challenging to be here in the now, or stay present and engaged with life around them.

True balance for an intuitive person means you are able to manage your intuitive gifts while also staying present and grounded. There are many mindfulness tools and exercises you can use to strengthen your ability to stay grounded. Perhaps the best tool of all is to spend time in nature. The human energy field is literally recharged by the healing vibration of trees and soil.

A trip to the park, a hike in the snow, or even time spent sitting under a tree are all revitalizing and can help you (or your intuitive child) counteract the frantic energy that abounds in our fast-paced society. While it's easy to let opportunities to spend time in nature pass you by, please remember the significant value it provides to your spirit. In fact, the more you acknowledge and develop your intuitive faculties, the more time you may want and need to spend in nature. Perhaps this is why so many intuitive and energetically sensitive people feel strongly connected to the earth and natural environments.

Easier Together

The tools and techniques presented in this chapter are ones you can use effectively on your own, which is great because you may already be at the point where being in large crowds and working with others is too exhausting or painful. However, it is easier to navigate this path if you are able to join in community with like-minded and like-gifted people. In the next chapter, we'll explore how finding community and mentorship can help strengthen and ground your intuition in a meaningful way.

4

Step Four:
Find Your Community

Seeking Guidance, Knowledge, and Support

"So, what do you think?" I'd just finished sharing some of my most recent experiences with the midwives who had been supporting me since my first pregnancy. We had developed a sweet sisterhood of support, and I appreciated their insight and guidance as I was learning to navigate my gifts.

"Niki, I think it may be helpful for you to begin taking some classes. Maybe study Reiki or Theta Healing. See where that experience leads you. But at least you'll be surrounded by people who understand what you're experiencing and may have helpful tools," one of them suggested without hesitation.

I love that type of direct guidance and support, so I signed up for the Reiki training. It was the most wonderful feeling in the world to walk into a room filled with other gifted intuitives. My heart opened up as I was greeted by the teaching assistants and introduced to the other students. I looked around and recognized that I was in the company of people who understood everything I was experiencing and could help me embrace my gifts rather than run from them like I had in the past. I took a seat in the middle of the room, happy to finally belong to a community of like-minded, like-hearted, and like-gifted souls. It was the first time I came to fully realize that we are not meant to be alone as we learn to navigate our intuitive gifts and use them with discernment.

In some indigenous cultures, intuitive children were prized for their great value to the community. They were trained from an early age by tribal teachers, priests, shamans, and chiefs. That is quite a contrast to what many of us experience today. Because we aren't well understood or don't fit in, we internalize feelings of confusion, shame, low self-esteem, anxiety, and alienation. There is no mentorship or training in schools, churches, or spiritual communities. Consequently, we have all these faculties and no idea what to do with them. For the sake of self-preservation (lest we be viewed as weird, foolish, delusional, or worse), we learn to suppress or hide our gifts. In school, we can feel marginalized by all kinds of labels. As adults, the resulting problems of inauthentic living build up inside of us. We feel alone with nowhere to turn and no one to understand us.

We were never meant to live this kind of secret life, keeping our deepest experiences hidden from sight. Fortunately, the global intuitive community is growing, as increasing numbers of people recognize their intuitive abilities. With this evolution and the reach of the Internet, it is no longer necessary for us to live isolated lives. There are communities of highly and energetically sensitive people, energy therapists and healers, psychics, mediums, shamans, lightworkers, intuitive natural healers, and many other types of intuitives. There are teachers, mentors, centers, events, support groups, and other resources… if we know where to find them.

Discovering a like-minded community is extremely important to help you thrive as an intuitive. Even if you don't want to develop your abilities, an intuitive community is essential in helping you understand who you are and how you can maintain vibrant health and wellness. For example, it's easy in everyday life to not take the time for necessary self-care (methods of self-care for intuitives are discussed in more detail in chapter six), unless you have people around you to inspire and motivate you. Even better, a community of intuitive people can help you find the resources you need, including professionals you can trust. You can learn from other people's experiences and even trade sessions if you are a practitioner.

It's important to know people who can relate to your experiences. There are so many things that come up in our lives, including visions, dreams, predictions, synchronicities, out-of-body experiences, encounters with guides or other realms—things that, let's face it, may seem strange to some people. But believe me, they won't seem strange to an intuitive community! It's not healthy to keep all those feelings to yourself. It's a wonderful experience to share who you are with a peer, mentor, or community that speaks your language! No one is in a better position to give you support, encouragement, or feedback, and to help you evaluate and understand your experiences. For some intuitive people, it is their first opportunity to truly be themselves.

If you are interested in developing your intuitive abilities, finding a like-minded community is indispensable to help you evolve. Although many people who have intuitive gifts try to shut them down because they are scared or have been discouraged by religious indoctrination, cultural myths, and prejudices, some intuitive people simply have no one to turn to for guidance in how to use their gifts. You can easily get "stuck" on your intuitive path without mentors, teachers, or peers to offer you guidance on your journey.

Harsh, But Much-Needed Guidance

I learned many valuable tools in these energy healing and intuition development classes, but I wasn't taught how to not take on the pains of other people. I was learning wonderful techniques, and feeling understood by others like me, but I wasn't really finding the mentorship or guidance I needed. I was being turned loose with all these skills and capabilities, but my needs as an intuitive empath weren't being addressed.

I was invited to a holiday party soon after my gifts first opened up, and suddenly my left breast started hurting. I knew that if I felt a pain like that, it meant that someone in the room had that pain, and it would stay with me until I spoke to that person. I knew of no other way to get the pain to go away. I walked around the party until the pain started throbbing and pulsing like a radar, and that's when I knew I had found the right person.

A holiday party is not the right time to tell a woman you can feel her breast cancer, but I decided to talk to her several days later. I told her a little about my work with intuitive energy and the process I experienced. She seemed open and curious. I told her my left breast had been hurting and it got stronger when I got close to her at the party, so perhaps she might want to check it out when she went to the doctor for her next check up.

Her eyes opened wide and she looked stunned. I could immediately tell that something was wrong, but I didn't know what. She said very little to me about what I had told her. In fact, from then on, she never spoke to me again. Any time I saw her socially, she would avoid me. Later, I found out that she had breast cancer, but she feared losing her job if people found out about her condition. No wonder she had that shocked look on her face!

After that incident, I was really lost. I knew I had to find a teacher to help me learn better ways to handle my experiences as an intuitive empath. There were no books about this topic at that time, and none of my teachers were able to help me *not* feel other people's pain.

That was when I discovered the book, *Positive Energy*, by Judith Orloff, M.D. She was on the medical faculty of UCLA where I had just finished my PhD! I can't tell you how thrilled I was to find someone with such academic credibility writing and speaking about energy and intuition. I found out she was offering a workshop in Sedona, AZ, and I paid a premium to sit in a front row seat so I could be sure she would see me when she did the Q&A session. It was expensive for me at the time, but I was determined to learn more about how to handle my gifts!

When it came time for the workshop, my daughter, who I was nursing, wasn't feeling well. I was so determined to learn more about my gift that I packed up my 8-month-old baby and we flew to Phoenix, AZ; then I rented a car and drove to Sedona. I couldn't wait to hear this doctor and author talk about how to *not* feel other people's energy in my body. I can't describe the anticipation I felt!

When I got there, I gave up my front row seat in case my baby started crying. This also meant that I forfeited the money I paid for the "premium" seat, because I sat in the back of the room instead. Still, I was the only African American in the room, and I was certainly the only one there with a baby, so I really stood out!

Not long after she started speaking, Judith Orloff scanned the room and looked straight at me. I couldn't believe she was talking to me first. She pointedly asked me, *"Why are YOU here?"* This was the moment I had been waiting for.

I explained that I came with my baby because I was desperate to understand how to use my gift wisely. I described my experience with the woman with the breast pain, and explained that I wanted to know how I could prevent situations like this from happening in the future. In a harsh tone, Dr. Orloff asked me, "And why do you think that woman wanted to know she had breast cancer?"

I said that I hadn't thought about that aspect of my revelation to her. I just knew it was the only way the pain in my body would go away. Dr. Orloff continued, in the same harsh tone, "Perhaps it was none of your business! Perhaps she didn't want to know!"

You could feel the audience tensing up. Everyone was staring at me. Dr. Orloff went on, "You think a lot of yourself, don't you? You think you're just going to heal the world, don't you?"

Needless to say, that wasn't the direction I had expected things to go. She never did address how not to feel other people's pain. Instead, she talked about the importance of discernment. It was the most shocking and embarrassing public put-down I had ever faced. Even the staff noticed that the encounter was a rough one. They apologized and gave me a full refund for my front-row seat! I felt frustrated and humiliated, and I still didn't understand why I was feeling people's pain or what I was or was not supposed to do or say.

In fact, this was the last incident before I made my decision to stop working as an intuitive empath. I started to pray to God to just please take this all away. I was getting too sick, while the people I was helping were getting better. I was a mom and I couldn't afford to have impaired health and energy levels.

I reasoned that maybe I could work with children and not get as sick as I did working with adults, and I quickly found that indeed I could help children with my work. As I was working with them, I found new ways to help prevent energetic sickness. Sometimes the children themselves gave me new ideas, energetically, as we worked together.

Of course, I didn't forget my experience with Dr. Orloff. To the contrary, I gradually began to understand that although the lesson had been a harsh one, it was also invaluable. My stubborn personality needed to understand the importance of discernment.

Ultimately, Dr. Orloff's lesson to me became part of the foundation of my work, the Innerlight Method that I developed, and my training. To this day, I greatly admire Dr. Judith Orloff for the powerful pioneering work she does, and am grateful for what she taught me.

Discernment and Boundaries

After my lesson with Dr. Orloff, I realized that just because I picked up something about someone didn't mean that person needed to know about it. As intuitives, there are many things we might discover that require discernment and discretion. What if we sense that someone is going to lose his or her job, or someone is cheating on their spouse, or even that someone might die?

We sometimes sense these things because we are sensitive to energy, and people's energy fields project the truth about them. Now I think of it like seeing your neighbors having an argument while walking your dog past their picture window. You would never approach them later and say, "Hey, how did that argument with your wife go?" We understand and respect the fact that that information wasn't meant for us.

Intuitive information works in that same way. On some level, we know what is not meant for us and when it is not appropriate for us to get involved. We may not be aware of this when we begin to develop our skills, but with practice, we can develop our intuitive discernment as well.

How do you create boundaries for the information you receive? The most important place to start is to take charge of your faculties so you do not receive information unless you intend to. In general, it's a good idea not to receive or share information with anyone who has not agreed to it first. It is unethical to do energy balancing with anyone who has not given you permission. (Or in the case of a child, a parent or guardian must give you permission.)

For example, it is not okay to psychically check up on your partner to see if they're cheating on you, or try to clear negative energy out of your angry friend's field without their permission. I am very strict about this point with my students and have asked people to leave the class if they practice energy work on someone without their knowledge and consent.

What do you do with the information you receive during a session with a client or someone who has asked you to give them intuitive information? One of the techniques I use is to ask if what I am considering sharing is *helpful, hopeful,* or *useful* for the other person. This was an important insight I learned from studying the work of Edgar Cayce.

It is always a good idea to ask Spirit or your guides if the information is meant to be shared. Sometimes you may get the answer that you are meant to share only part of the information you have received, or that you should share it later with the person. It is not unusual for me to share less than half of what I see in a session. Sometimes I will ask,

"Of all that I have been shown, what is the most important information for me to share?"

Finally, I mentioned earlier that you can set boundaries on the type of information you want to receive. I know that in my early work as an intuitive, I used to receive more ominous information about things such as job losses or illnesses, but as I have evolved, I now receive more optimistic information. I now deliberately set an intention to receive instructive information that can best help my client achieve their highest purpose in life.

As you find a community of intuitive peers and mentors, you will be able to share your experiences and challenges with topics such as discernment, boundaries, how to manage your capabilities, and much more.

Initially, it can be fascinating to experiment with your abilities: to give readings or energy sessions for people and see that your information is accurate or that your work is helping other people. It is exciting—and seductive. In my own work, I have learned to remove the idea of myself as the doer. I developed the Innerlight Method to work with the client's own self-healing ability, rather than any healing ability of mine. I believe all healing is self-healing, and as practitioners, we merely facilitate and witness the self-healing process. I prefer to avoid the word "healer" as much as possible, and I don't accept the praise or the responsibility for any changes or shifts my clients experience. They are doing the healing work; I simply guide the process.

Your ego can get involved in these early stages, and you can get caught in a cycle of craving validation for your gifts. A good teacher, and willing peers, can help you avoid these and other pitfalls.

Choose Teachers Carefully

It's important to be discerning in your choice of intuitive teachers. There are people who may recognize your abilities and want to take you under their wing, but ultimately may have an imbalanced psychic relationship with you. For example, a woman from my yoga community saw that I had gifts and offered to mentor me with weekly meetings. Eventually she became adamant about telling me how to live my life, to the point of insisting on what house I should buy! Her input became very intrusive and I was forced to terminate our relationship.

I made decisions early on when using my gifts that I regret to this day, giving too much of my power to her and thinking that everything she was "seeing" for me was the absolute truth. Fortunately, I was way too stubborn to let anyone tell me what to do for too long, and I give no one that power in my life today.

Again, the lessons I learned were valuable ones. (Even when you don't choose the right teacher, the experience can be useful.) Eventually, I learned two things: to not give too much power to others, and also to not let clients give too much power to *me*. For example, as I built my practice working with children, I found that sometimes parents would become too dependent on receiving input from me, such as asking me what schools their children should go to, and so on. I learned that when your intuitive information is accurate, some people will even want you to tell them what side of the bed to sleep on!

A good teacher will develop your sense of self-empowerment rather than encourage you to rely on him or her. As you recognize and explore your skills, it can start to shake things up in your life. You may wake up new abilities, or find that things begin to shift in your work or relationships. You may find yourself drawn to different nutrition or lifestyle activities as your energy field clears and purifies. This transitional time can be an exciting and positive time if you have knowledgeable and encouraging guidance from someone who cares about your well-being and has a high level of integrity.

When you search for classes, groups, or teachers, consider your personal learning style, needs, and interests. Do you feel more comfortable being anonymous? If so, then an online group might be a good place to start. Do you prefer in-person, hands-on help? Then look for local mentors. Are you interested in afterlife experiences, dream interpretation, astral travel, energy awareness, working with crystals, connecting with nature, or other fields of study? Choose books or online courses that introduce you to these concepts and attend workshops with teachers that resonate with you.

There are some fabulous teachers online and in many communities across the country. There are so many great people I admire and respect, such as Judith Orloff, MD, Sara Wiseman, Larry Dossey, MD, Cyndi Dale, Donna Eden, and Caroline Myss, to name just a few. Think about where you want to start, take a leap of faith, and find a teacher and a community to support you on your journey!

Intuitive Teacher Checklist

I wish someone had given me a checklist like this to use as a guide to find a teacher who was best suited to my needs. It would have saved me a lot of the drama that can easily be avoided.

A good intuitive teacher or mentor will:

- Help you understand and express your intuitive gifts
- Help you practice spiritual discernment in how you use your gifts
- Have strong boundaries in their own work and teach you about developing strong boundaries
- Establish ethical boundaries for doing energy work *only* with people who have given their permission
- Practice regular self-care and energy hygiene themselves and teach self-care and energy hygiene
- Be more concerned about developing your own personal power than getting you to admire or rely on their power
- Not be primarily focused on selling you products or services

- Not be threatened by your abilities and uncomfortable with the idea that your abilities may equal or exceed their own

- Allow you to have your own spiritual path, even when it is different from theirs

- Not try to manage your life or feel they know more about what's best for you than you do

- Encourage you to be an autonomous—an independent thinker—and allow you to work with other teachers to explore and study other methods and approaches rather than saying their system is the "only" one

- Direct you to trust your own in-dwelling sense of knowing and wisdom

- Be emotionally stable with a manageable life and no active addictions or untreated mental illness*

Intuitive people, just as any other group, may require treatment for mental illness. A good teacher will exhibit strong mental and emotional health and also be aware of any problems that come up with students. I have asked students to seek professional help when needed, and these students went on to become remarkable intuitives.

Sometimes intuitive experiences can create confusion about one's mental health, although that is changing as more mental health professionals are exposed to intuitive abilities and experiences. Please take your mental health seriously and seek the support of licensed professionals when necessary.

Staying Well in Community

As you've seen in my story and probably experienced in your own life, being in large crowds can be draining and painful for empaths. It's definitely helpful to seek the support of like-minded communities and mentors who can guide you based on their experiences. In addition to outside guidance, it's important to have a set of self-care tools that help you engage with others and your life in a much easier, healthier way. In the next section, you'll be introduced to several techniques you can use right away to regulate your energy field and intuitive abilities.

5

Step Five: Clear Your Field

The Art of Mastering Energy

Ugh. I put my hand on my stomach and asked, "Is this my pain?"

"*No,*" I heard from my inner guidance.

The pain had been there for days, since the music festival I'd attended, and I didn't know what to do to release it. Normally, when I was in a crowd, I had a way of identifying whose pain I was picking up and releasing it by sharing a message with them. But I'd been unable to do that and now I was suffering.

I was lying in bed, wondering what my next step was when I heard my inner voice say, "*Get up and go to yoga.*"

What? I feel like crap and you want me to do yoga? I don't know if I could make it through a class.

"Go, and feel better."

With that bit of encouragement, I threw on my yoga clothes and headed to class.

I was right. I barely made it through the class. It was a Kundalini yoga set, which meant a lot of breath work and exercises designed to move and balance energy in the body. At one point, I was doing a twisting solar plexus exercise that hurt so bad, I thought I might throw up. As I began to get up to go to the bathroom, my inner voice said, *"Just keep going. It's okay..."*

By the end of the class, the stomach ache was gone. I was so amazed that I hung back to talk to the teacher after class. When I told her what I'd been experiencing and how the class helped, she nodded and explained that the yoga set she taught that day was designed to help clear and recharge the magnetic field. "The twisting exercises clear old energy and the outward stretching moves recharge your electromagnetic field," is what she told me.

"That's amazing! Thank you for explaining this to me!" I almost bounced out of that yoga studio. Not only did I feel better, but now I had a new set of tools I could use to take care of myself.

Until now, your intuitive experience has probably been mostly an unconscious one. If you think of your intuition as a vehicle that carries you through life, you have essentially been getting dragged down the road by the car's bumper! But now that you've identified and claimed your power, you're in the driver's seat. Learning to master your intuition doesn't happen automatically; instead it is a lifelong process of awareness, intention, and action.

A reminder before we go further: if you really want to manage and develop your intuition, you have to be willing to suspend disbelief. In other words, you may find at times that you have to act "as-if," even if you're not sure about what you're doing. This is unfamiliar territory and it doesn't help that we have all been taught to doubt things we can't experience with our five physical senses.

You may think that these exercises are too easy because they involve only awareness and consciousness. Again, this is prior conditioning at work, because it is not always easy to maintain awareness and focus. And who says everything has to be hard? Be careful of old ideas that stand between you and your intuition.

In the beginning of accessing your intuition, it may feel like it is only your imagination at work or that you are making things up. If you were taught to believe that imagination or visualization isn't important or "real," it may be difficult initially to embrace the idea that intuition often operates through mental images and symbols. I encourage you to take this important leap of faith. Over time, you will develop a strong ability to focus your thoughts and expand your access to the messages you receive from your higher consciousness, that aspect of you that is all-knowing.

Clients always ask me, "How can it be this easy? How do I know something real is happening?" When I teach intuition development or energy balancing techniques, clients say, "Oh my God, I felt that in my body! Or am I just making it up?" We don't trust ourselves because of how we've been taught. I tell them, "No, you weren't making it up. You were just engaging with another aspect of your real self that you can access with your intuitive senses, just not your physical ones."

To make progress, you will need to entertain the possibility that mastering your intuition can be this easy! What's been missing until now has been a clear understanding of what you are experiencing and the application of intentioned, focused awareness. As we discussed in chapter three, intuitive information comes to you through your energy field. To use your intuitive gifts with intention and purpose, you need to learn to balance, organize, and maintain the health of your energy field. This involves:

- Understanding energy
- Managing your energy field
- Maintaining strong energetic boundaries
- Clearing your field of debris and imbalances, such as energetic blending

Let's look at each of these areas and how they can help you master your intuitive experiences.

Understanding Energy

To master intuition, you need to take responsibility for your energy field through sustained focused attention. This is because intuition, like all things, is energy. Your intuition comes to you through your energy field. Instead of just experiencing what comes, you are now learning to become an active, conscious participant in the experience so that you can have a direct relationship with your inner guidance.

We tend to think of energy as unknowable, when in fact we all know a great deal about energy. The energetic nature of reality is not just a theory; it is very real. Physicists have confirmed that this world cannot be perceived with our eyes alone. But you don't need to be a physicist to experience the effects of energetic systems.

We respond, often automatically, to certain colors, sounds, people, and places in various ways without thinking about the fact that we are really responding to the energy of those colors, sounds, people, and places. Think about how you feel after a meditation or a day spent in a beautiful place in nature. Or think about the difference in how you feel on a sunny day versus a rainy one, in a cluttered house versus a clean one, when you hear rhythmic ocean waves versus loud traffic sounds, or soft classical music versus loud dance music.

We can't see this energy, but we know it's there! From quantum physics, we know that everything is made of energy, including our thoughts and feelings. The current model of traditional Western medicine is built on the 200-year-old Newtonian model, which views the human body as a grand machine with parts that simply need to be fixed when broken in order for human beings to be well.

But times are changing and most of us now know that we are much more than glorified machines. The science of energy medicine, also called vibrational medicine, is based on the Einsteinian model that views all matter—including the human body, as an expression of energy. From this perspective, we are intricate, sophisticated networks of energy fields that integrate our physical, mental, spiritual, and emotional bodies.

We each have a unique energetic profile that transcends our physical body and includes our unique passions, destiny, and even the story of our ancestry. Our behaviors, thoughts, belief patterns, and various factors in our physical bodies and our environment can all affect our energy field.

When your energy centers are blocked or out of balance, energy doesn't flow well and various disturbances and challenges can result, including depression, anxiety, tension, and aggression, as well as physical diseases or illnesses. In energy medicine, disease and illness states are a cry for unresolved emotion and trauma to be faced, resolved, and released.

Energy medicine gives us a method to identify where emotions and thought energy are trapped in the body, so we can recognize the mental or emotional block, accept it, forgive it, and release it.

Energy Balancing for Intuitives

I train Innerlight Method practitioners to maintain a state of higher consciousness (focused awareness) and to anchor higher vibrational frequencies of pure love, unity, and forgiveness for their clients. At this higher energetic vibration, Innerlight practitioners can help intuitive people elevate their own consciousness to perform innate functions of balancing, self-healing, and managing their intuitive abilities.

When we access this higher level of consciousness, we are reminded of the truth of who we are. We know that what holds us back from growth is not real. We can heal the lower vibrations, or the blocked energy of unhealthy thoughts, beliefs, resentments, and trauma that can keep us from functioning at our best or is expressed as disease. It is a common misconception that energy practitioners heal their clients. In fact, the energy body heals itself. Energy medicine merely guides the process.

When I use the Innerlight Method with intuitive adults or children, they quickly find they can manage their intuitive abilities so that they can function better in their daily lives. Once they are able to live, study, and work more effectively, without being energetically overloaded, they often choose to further develop their intuition and create exciting new directions in their lives.

You don't need to see an energy practitioner to get started on learning to manage your energy, since there is a lot you can do on your own. But first, you will need to get to know your energy field.

Working With Your Energy Field

Being an empath deeply impacts one's ability to work in professions that involve significant contact with groups or individuals. Empathic ministers, physicians, teachers, motivational speakers, psychologists, and many other helping professionals must learn to manage their fields so they can speak in front of groups or work closely with sick or stressed individuals without being energetically drained.

Performers and artists have similar challenges if they don't know how to do effective energetic preparation. They perform for audiences and crowds, become overloaded and depleted, then have to work with managers, dancers, a band, or fans, and perhaps get back out on the road again without any energetic relief. They energetically blend with dozens, hundreds, or even thousands of people, absorbing all that energy without any knowledge of how to clear it. Is it any wonder some resort to harmful self-numbing behaviors?

Performing or speaking is a good example of when energy management is especially critical, but you don't have to be a speaker or performer to become energetically overloaded. Many intuitive people, adults and children alike, turn to abusive or self-abusive behaviors to relieve energy overload that could easily be taken care of with energy management techniques. (This is not to say that there might not be a mental health component as well; sometimes that is a factor that needs to be addressed.) The bottom line is that many intuitive people suffer needlessly from energetic overload—or even quit professions they love, when there are other solutions.

Feel Your Field

To begin experiencing your own energy field, stretch out your arms and simply ask yourself, "How far does my energy field extend right now?" Feel, see, hear, taste, smell, think or imagine where the edges or boundaries of your field are. Trust whatever answer comes to you.

Generally, a healthy energy field extends an arm's length around you in all directions, but remember that nothing is ever fixed. Your energy is a fluid dance around you, constantly changing based on your intentions, thoughts, emotions, experiences, and circumstances. At this moment, do you think your field extends to within inches of your body? Several feet from you? Is it much larger than that?

Now ask yourself one more question: "What is a healthy distance for my energy field at this time?" When the answer comes, feel, see, hear, taste, smell, think or imagine your energy boundaries adjusting to the guidance you have been given.

Simple, right? Two questions are all it takes to adjust the size of your energy field.

Different activities or environments call for different energy fields. For example, if you are about to speak or be the center of attention, you may want to expand your energy field to create a "big" presence. Ever wonder how charismatic people command attention? By creating large, strong energy fields!

Now let's say you are in a situation where you just want to "blend in," perhaps at someone else's celebration where you don't want to be a distraction. Just contract your energy field so it is close around you.

Adjusting your energy is an ongoing dance. Think of your energy field like clothing. You don't dress the same way every day no matter what you're doing. You don't wear a suit to the park or a t-shirt to the White House. The same is true of your energy field. You want to learn to adjust your field to whatever is optimal for the situation you are in. When your environment changes, your energetic field needs to change.

Think about how you check the time or the weather throughout the day. You don't stress or think about it too much, just enough to keep your day on track and to stay prepared. That's how you want to think about energy management—as something you stay aware of in order to be prepared. It takes practice! You won't learn it in a day. You will need to find ways to remind yourself at first, but eventually it can become second nature.

If you are speaking to a crowd, you may want your energetic "wingspan" to fill the whole room. If your energetic field fills the entire room, you are in a better position to radiate hope and strength to your audience while maintaining enough energetic distance for yourself. This allows you to effect change without absorbing the energies of your audience, leaving you exhausted. If you find yourself drained after a presentation, you will know it is because you didn't adequately prepare yourself.

Remember that you are not just your physical body taking up space—you are your physical body *plus* your energetic body. Highly sensitive people need more space around them, which is why crowds can be so challenging. But when you learn to adapt your energy field to the circumstance, such as by energetically making more room for yourself, you can enjoy almost any environment you're in.

One way to increase your awareness of your energy field is to simply watch or feel how it changes. For example, when I get to the 110 Freeway in Los Angeles on my way home and start seeing trees, I know I will soon be at my house which is close to the Angeles National Forest, and I can feel my energy field open up and expand. When I feel concerned or anxious, I can feel my energy field shrinking or tightening. As long as I am aware of what is happening, I can choose to just observe or to consciously change my field.

Use your intuition! Allow your energetic body to show you what you need. It will know better than you. Notice how it shifts and how it feels to you. You can always use intention to adjust it.

Preparation, Not Protection

Sometimes people talk about "protecting" their energy field or blocking out bad energy. There are all kinds of ideas out there for keeping yourself "safe" from harmful energy. I don't think that a fear-based defensiveness is a healthy way to approach consciousness. For one thing, it takes too much energy! And if you are always blocking, fighting, and protecting, you can cut off access to positive energy and connections that you want to invite in.

If we are always thinking about building walls to keep energy out, we run the risk of sealing ourselves off from other people and many of the joys and wonders of life. We can close off our energy so much that it negatively affects relationships, bonding, and other people's perceptions of who we are.

When you see someone who seems unable to trust people or to feel the love that is being offered to them, often their energy field is rigidly closed off. We need to be able to exchange energy with each other in a healthy way so we can relate and know the truth about each other.

Instead of walling off our energy with a fearful attitude, I prefer to think of the ring of energy around us as a kind of door. We don't generally think of doors as protecting us from evil predators, although they sometimes do that. More often, we use doors to maintain boundaries. You may think, "I'm going to close my office door to protect myself from what's on the other side." However, the ultimate goal is to create a quiet space for yourself and to exercise your control of who and what enters.

You can use the "energy door" image in the same way. You can choose to close the door when you want to conserve your energy, for those times when you don't want anything to get in or out. You can open the door when you want to really connect to people you love. And you can use a screen door option when you want to let the breeze (love, good intentions) in, but keep the bugs (energetic chaos) out! This is the option I use most of the time with the intention of letting in what is for my highest good and keeping out what isn't.

Nothing is permanent. You can open, close, or screen your energy door whenever you want. I use the screen door option frequently when I speak. If I am in a place that is loud and overwhelming, I usually close my energetic door because I want to be sealed in. If I am in a hostile negotiating session where I don't want people to "read" me, or if I am with people I'm not sure I can trust, I close the energetic door. But I always do so with the awareness that it is just a closed door, not a locked or guarded one! I can open the door whenever I want.

Healthy Energy Boundaries

By learning to maintain a strong energy field with healthy energy boundaries, many of my clients experience freedom for the first time in their lives. They are finally able to socialize and serve others without feeling energetically overwhelmed or depleted. From this empowered position, intuitive people can use their gifts in powerful ways to change the world!

Everywhere you turn there are heartbreaking stories of the hardships of others. While it's natural to respond with expressions of compassion, generosity, and kindness, many empathic adults and children feel a deep inner pressure to make everything okay for everyone. If you or your child is an intuitive empath, you can begin to feel and act out these feelings of anxiety even though they did not originate from your own experience.

Establishing healthy energetic boundaries enables you to act with compassion for others without absorbing or carrying their energy and emotions.

Energetic boundaries help us to keep our energy or electromagnetic field in balance while keeping other people's energy out. When we have healthy energy boundaries, we feel balanced, clear, and light, no matter what is taking place around us. Maintaining healthy energetic boundaries is especially important for intuitive empaths like me—people who tend to absorb or take on another's feelings, emotions, or illnesses in their own body.

The best gift you can give yourself is to learn to establish your own energetic boundaries and teach your children to do the same. According to Cyndi Dale, author of *Energetic Boundaries: How to Stay Protected and Connected in Work, Love, and Life,* "Energetic boundaries border our spiritual selves and support our true nature. When created and managed correctly, they make sure that our real selves—not the ideas, thoughts, and beliefs that aren't us—are in charge of our lives. They share information with the world telling everyone exactly who we are, what we want, and how they can treat us."

In working with my clients, I have found a wide variety of problems related to energetic boundary issues, such as attracting predators or abusive relationships, having trouble holding on to money, and experiencing general issues with self-esteem. Most importantly, if you have compromised, damaged, or non-existent energetic boundaries, you are highly susceptible to absorbing other people's energy and carrying it in your own body.

Since intuitive and empathic people are already spiritually wired to absorb and process a heightened level of information, not having healthy boundaries allows everything to come in unfiltered. This, in turn, fries the nervous system and ends up being the "invisible cause" of many of the moods, behaviors, focus, attention, learning, and social interaction problems that are so often misdiagnosed as something else.

In the Innerlight Method, I identify four types of energy boundary issues, which I'll share with you now.

Too Open Boundaries

An energy field that is too open allows other people to impress their thoughts, feelings, and moods onto you. People whose energy boundaries are too open can end up feeling another person's physical illnesses, pains, and emotions in their body. They can walk into a room where there has been an argument or a situation and fully absorb all of that energy and start feeling sick or depressed.

People with boundaries that are too open can be highly impressionable or susceptible to subliminal programming and subtle media marketing, making them think that they want to buy something as if it was their own idea rather than a suggestion coming from outside of them! Companies that hire psychologists to influence people actively look for ways to cross over people's energetic boundaries and influence them to make purchasing decisions that aren't necessarily in their best interest. Having healthy boundaries allows all of the decisions you make and thoughts you are thinking to be your own.

Too Rigid Boundaries

Rigid energy boundaries are similar to a scar or a scab, or a hard surface that forms to cover a wound. It's a protective mechanism for people who have experienced heartbreak, disappointment, or trauma. As an attempted protection mechanism to keep from getting hurt, a person subconsciously thickens their energy boundary to the point where nothing gets in.

People in your life can be helpful and express love, compassion, and joy, but because your energy boundaries are thick and rigid, you may be unable to perceive and interpret the emotions coming toward you as benevolent. Likewise, a person with very rigid boundaries could attempt to express kindness, love, and joy, but not be able to transmit that communication effectively because their energetic boundary is too thick.

Nonexistent Boundaries

People with nonexistent energy boundaries have a hard time knowing where their energy stops and other people's begins. To some energy practitioners, the nonexistent boundary looks like a thin, wispy cloud that's starting to dissipate: there is no fully-formed energy field. People with nonexistent boundaries tend to insert themselves too much into others' lives and conversations. They come across as being really pushy because they don't know when they are supposed to back off.

Children without boundaries typically need to crash into things. They don't understand how hard they are touching people because they have no sense of personal space. They step on others' toes a lot, literally and figuratively. Their play is too rough, although they are not intentionally trying to hurt anyone. They just have no sense of where they are in time or space in relation to other people. People with nonexistent energy boundaries have a hard time making and keeping friends and establishing relationships because they can be difficult to be around.

Shattered Boundaries

This type of damaged boundary feels like static electricity when I work with it. Typically a person with a shattered energy boundary has experienced a significant trauma or violation, not only through physical, emotional, or sexual abuse, but also through serious accidents. If a person has been in a terrible car crash, has fallen, experienced a significant trauma, or suffered a brain injury where the body perceives the assault as a violation or trauma to the field, the energy field can be shattered.

Do any of these conditions sound familiar? An Innerlight Method session can be highly effective to help you repair your boundaries. You can also repair them yourself by setting positive intentions, seeing your energy field in your mind's eye, forgiving yourself and all others for anything related to your energy boundary situation, and witnessing your higher self restoring a healthy, balanced energy boundary.

Energetic Blending

If you're feeling someone else's physical or emotional pain, thoughts, or ideas in your body, mind, or energy field, you might be experiencing energetic (or empathic) blending, where two or more people's energy fields are overlapping. This usually happens with the intent to help and support another person, but ends up causing a drain on one person's energy "bank account."

Energetic blending is a type of energy exchange that occurs commonly between two people when there is an energetic transfer of information. The information is usually passed from the stronger or more vital person to the weaker one, but it can happen between any two people. It can be healthy or unhealthy depending on the type of information being transferred.

The transfer of love, positive intentions, or useful ideas is a good thing—we want to keep our energy fields open enough to experience positive blending with the world around us. However, when we find ourselves experiencing the physical and emotional pains, fears, resentments, or grief of others, the result is unhealthy. We can energetically blend with people we know or with strangers, although it most commonly happens with people we already know. The energetic blend can occur over major life events such as a death, or over small daily occurrences such as a minor disagreement at work. They can be fleeting or lasting episodes.

An example of unhealthy empathic blending is when a doctor or healthcare provider is overly empathic and they blend with their patients. If the doctor's energy field is weakened for any reason, the unhealthy states of their patients can affect the doctor's health as they are energetically transferred to him/her. This is a common cause of depression, burnout, and fatigue among healing professionals.

These kinds of energetic attachments rarely happen because of someone's intent to harm you. Usually, we have to energetically agree to the transfer because, on some level, we do experience a benefit. We often are not aware that energetic blending is occurring, although as we learn to pay closer attention, we can become more familiar with how it feels.

We clear energetic blending with the Innerlight Method and there are also ways you can clear it yourself. (See the "Energetic Blending Colors" exercise and the "Is This Mine?" exercise in the six clearing exercises that begin on the following section)

Becoming aware of energetic blending is a powerful first step to keeping your energy field clear. Sometimes it is necessary to heal issues of codependency as well, especially if you have abuse or addiction in your family background. If you are intuitive and have codependent tendencies, you are doubly predisposed to unhealthy energetic blending.

If your parents had poor energetic boundaries, you may also have difficulty with boundaries. You may have learned as a child to take on the burdens of your parents, for example, as a survival mechanism. You may have taken on a "martyr" identity as someone who feels other people's pain and can't do anything about it, or a "controller" role, as someone who manages the circumstances for everyone, or you may have taken on a "hero" or "savior" role as someone who solves other people's problems.

Sometimes intuitives who have taken on the "savior" role transfer that approach into healing, believing they can save others and taking responsibility for the healing results, when in reality, all healing is self-healing. Healing professionals and practitioners merely guide the process. An intuitive or healer who hasn't healed their own codependency issues can disempower others and distance them from their own ability to heal.

The word "healing" itself can be misleading, as we have come to view it as a process done by other people or things "for" or "to" us. Although the word sometimes can't be avoided, I don't want to take on the identity of "healer" when I work with my clients. In the Innerlight Method, I witness the healing work that clients do—I don't do it myself. I utilize my connection to the Divine as a method of communication and guidance, but the client's connection to the Divine is their source of healing. I am not the source. This keeps our relationship balanced as well. I am not putting myself "above" the client in any way, and the client does not have to depend on me to access healing and wellness.

If we bring codependency into our intuitive work, those roles of martyr, savior, controller, etc., will act as magnets that attract unhealthy energetic blending. We will take on a lot of energetic debris, just as I did when I absorbed all the energy from my church congregation, and we will make ourselves sick. If you feel you have codependent tendencies, find a professional or support group to help you learn to maintain good personal boundaries, which will also help you keep strong energetic boundaries.

Exercises to Clear Your Field

Below are six exercises you can use to help you clear and strengthen your energy field. There are many other methods available to you as well. Books such as *Self-Care for the Self-Aware: A Guide for Highly Sensitive People, Empaths, Intuitives, and Healers* by Dave Markowitz, and *Whose Stuff is This? Finding Freedom from the Thoughts, Feelings and Energy of Those Around You* by Yvonne Perry also have techniques and strategies you can use to keep your energy field healthy.

Remember that throughout the exercises I've included here, you are acting "as-if" the information you receive is accurate, until you have enough experience to know it is so. You are accessing the Superconscious, your Higher Self, or Divine Source (however you view it) for intuitive knowledge, as well as for your highest good and benefit.

#1- Energy Circuit Exercise

Running an energy circuit helps to clear your field and also balance it, as it symbolically unites feminine, right-brained energy (also associated in many cultures with Mother Earth), and masculine, left-brained energy (associated with Father Sun). When we run an energy circuit, we clear out any excess debris from our energy field and invite fresh new energy in.

Step 1: The first part of the circuit begins by visualizing yourself drawing fresh feminine energy from the earth up through your left foot and through your pelvic area or root chakra. This can be seen as white light. Then visualize the excess energy that you want to clear from your field as going down from your pelvic area, through your right leg, and exiting your right foot back into the earth.

Step 2: Now you will engage the masculine energy, or the light of the sun. Visualize sun energy coming down through the crown of your head and going in a straight line through the center of your body and the center of all your chakras.

Step 3: Now join the circuits at your pelvic area, or the root chakra, where the feminine and masculine energies meet. Visualize any excess energy exiting down your right leg and into the earth.

Energy Circuit Tips

As you witness the two circuits, see energy blocks and debris move out of your body through your right foot. This unwanted energy is replaced by the fresh energy of light and love from the earth and sun. Whenever a blockage is cleared, it leaves a void, and it's important to visualize yourself filling the void with love and light.

#2- Empathic Blending Colors Exercise

Step 1: Close your eyes and project a mental picture of your energy body, as if it were a holographic image facing you and you are looking at yourself.

Step 2: Ask, "What color is my energy bubble, or energy field at this time?" The color is always changing depending on your wellness, state of spiritual connection, and many other factors, so whatever color you are seeing simply represents the present.

Step 3: Scan your energy field or bubble and look to see if there are any specks of other colors in your field. You may see no specks, a few, or many.

Step 4: Ask yourself if those specks represent people you are blending with energetically. If the answer is no, ask if you are blending energetically with anyone at this time. If the answer is again no, thank your Divine Source and simply see your energy field clearing using the Energy Circuit Exercise.

Step 5: If the answer is yes, you can also ask who the colors represent, which may give you some idea of the energetic blending you are prone to (such as with your family, co-workers, etc.). You may get a name or image of a person, or a letter or sound, or some other signal that may represent someone you know in your life.

Step 6: Say the names of the people or simply state, "Any people I am energetically blended with…" and add the Forgiveness Statement: "In the spirit of unity and unconditional love, I now witness as we allow complete forgiveness of ourselves and each other to set us free from this unhealthy energetic blending. I witness as I release you from my energetic field in the highest and best way with harm to none."

Step 7: Watch as the colors dissolve out of your field and the energetic blending disappears.

Step 8: You can repeat the process for every person or speck of color if you wish. When you are finished, see your energy field as having only the color you started with that represents your field.

#3- "Is This Mine?" Exercise

Step 1: This is a very basic exercise that should become second nature for you. It is simply asking the question, "Is this mine?" so you can learn to distinguish what's coming from your own being and what belongs to someone else. For example, if you are experiencing a troubling thought or an emotion you can't shake, or a physical illness that seems unusual, ask yourself, "Is this mine?" We have been taught to assume that everything is ours, but as an intuitive, you need to get in the habit of asking the question to avoid taking on someone else's energy.

Step 2: Wait for the answer: either yes or no. You can watch or feel for signs in your body or synchronicities in your life that give you the answer. You also can use a pendulum or muscle testing. This is also a good way to start developing your spiritual language or the way that your Divine Source communicates with you.

Step 3: If the answer is no (this is not yours), use the Forgiveness Statement from the Energetic Blending Colors exercise and the Energy Circuit exercise to clear the energy.

Note: Remember that you can experience energetic blending from the world around you, or from the "collective," such as through media or social conditioning. As you become aware of energetic blending, you may find you have to manage your media and online information flow more carefully. Turn your devices off and get out into nature as much as you can.

#4- Energy Trash Can Exercise

Step 1: When you pick up too much energetic debris, you may start to feel anxious, additional pressure, irritated, or aggressive. Often we don't realize what is making us "bubble up." So get in the habit of focusing on your personal "energetic trash can." You can think of it the way your trash can looks on a computer screen.

Step 2: Stand up, close your eyes, and scan your body. Get quiet and ask your body, "How energetically full am I right now?" See or imagine a line or color on your body that tells you how full you are of energetic debris. For example, you may see or feel that you are full up to your knees, waist, chest, or even over your head. If you have just cleared your energy field yourself or during an energy session, you may find that your trash can is close to the floor or empty. When your trash can fills above the stomach area, I have found that my clients start to have physical symptoms related to energetic overload. If they wait until they feel filled up to the chest or neck area, that's when clients experience behavior meltdowns or paralyzing anxiety.

Step 3: Inhale, filling your belly like a hot air balloon. Next, exhale, releasing all the air until your stomach is "flat as a pancake" trying to make your belly button touch your spine. As you breathe, lace your fingers with you palms face down at the top of your head. Make a sweeping motion from head to toe and imagine yourself pushing the energy down and out of your body, emptying your energetic trash can. Make as many sweeps as you need and visualize doing the same thing in the back of your body.

Step 4: Once you have emptied your trash can, you can imagine the sound of the trash leaving your body (just as it does on your computer when you "empty" the trash bin). Now feel light energy filling your whole body from the crown down to your toes. Then push this light energy out through the energy bubble or field surrounding your body.

Note: Remember to pay attention to signs that you may be getting overloaded. Note that different environments will cause different energetic responses and sensations. This exercise works well with children. You can teach them to do it themselves when they feel stressed or anxious.

#5- Three-Step Energy Adjuster Exercise

This exercise is described in greater detail earlier in this chapter.

Step 1: Stretch out your arms and simply ask yourself, "How far does my energy field extend right now?" Feel, see, hear, taste, smell, think, or imagine where the edges or boundaries of your field are. Trust whatever answer comes to you.

Step 2: Ask yourself, "What is a healthy distance for my energy field at this time?"

Step 3: When the answer comes, feel, see, hear, taste, smell, think, or imagine your energy boundaries adjusting to the guidance you have been given.

#6- Open Door/Closed Door/Screen Door Exercise

Step 1: Imagine your energy field as a door that protects you from unwanted energetic input or influence. You can choose a closed door, a screen door, or an open door. Each choice symbolizes the type of energetic boundaries you wish to establish in a given situation.

Step 2: Depending on your circumstances, see yourself closing your energy field door if you want to create a strong energetic barrier for a time to keep unhelpful energy out. This can be particularly helpful if you are in the company of someone you find untrustworthy or energetically draining. It's also helpful when you visit large, crowded places. See yourself opening the door if you want to encourage deep energetic exchange with those nearest and dearest to you. Picture yourself using a screen door if you want to allow in some helpful energy, but keep out anything that is not for your highest good. I usually default to setting my energy boundary as a screened door. I want to be able to relate and connect with others, while leaving all of their energetic debris and pain outside my door. Remember to adjust your door again when circumstances change.

Of all the energy management techniques presented here, I consistently find that my clients respond best to the Open Door/Screen Door/Closed Door technique. One of the most important reasons is that it eliminates the idea of protecting oneself with shields or barriers. It becomes exhausting to think constantly of defending oneself against the world. This technique is just as simple and casual as opening the doors of your home to invited guests and closing the doors of your home to unwelcomed visitors.

Exercise: Energy Field Awareness

For the next several days, set an intention to visit places that you usually find energetically draining. For example, you may actively avoid indoor shopping malls because you feel overwhelmed or nauseated after a short time. This time when you visit, practice one or two of the energy field techniques presented in this chapter. Journal your experiences and notice whether you find it easier to enjoy places or people that were previously difficult to endure.

A New Way of Interacting with the World

These tools will help you begin to clear your own field and master your energy, especially when you feel overwhelmed. Making them daily practices will change your life. In the next chapter, we will cover additional energy hygiene practices that will help you not only clear your field but keep it strong and healthy.

6

Step Six:
Practice Energy Hygiene

Self-Care Secrets for Intuitives

It had been a long day of back-to-back client sessions, and I was completely wiped out. I dragged myself across the parking lot and into the community kitchen at the Healing Arts Center. I was sipping some water and preparing a snack when Dr. Kenny, my mentor and colleague, walked into the kitchen.

She took one look at me and said, "Niki, it looks like you've had a really long day with clients."

"Mmmmmhmmmmmm..." the murmured acknowledgment was all I could muster.

"How about you take the rest of the afternoon off and go home and take a nice Epsom salt bath!" It was more of a loving directive than a suggestion.

"Well, I have…" I started. But then I looked up at her and knew she meant business and that it was true: I was at the end of my energetic rope for the day.

"Okay. Thank you for looking out for me." I smiled at her and went home.

Once I was in my bathroom, I turned on the faucet, poured an entire four-pound bag of Epsom salt into the tub, lit six candles, and dropped my tired body into the hot water.

"Mmmmmmmmmm…" I literally moaned with the relief I could feel on the horizon. She was right. I needed some time to myself… to be quiet and restore.

I had no idea how powerful an Epsom salt bath could be until I got out of the tub and noticed how all of the tension had left my body…and it felt like my energetic strength had been restored. It wasn't until much later that I found out that Epsom salt is actually magnesium, which is known to reset our energetic field.

If you are like most people, you greatly underestimate the impact that the state of your energy field has on your life and your health. When you feel sick, stressed, burned out, or otherwise unable to function well, you probably look for causes in your life circumstances or your physical, emotional, or mental health. But how often do you think to check your energetic health? All health and illnesses begin in the energetic field. If you can maintain health and balance there you will have a strong foundation for wellness, physically, emotionally, and mentally. Through increased conscious awareness, you can take important steps to clear yourself and claim optimal well-being in every area of your life.

As an intuitive, empath, or highly sensitive person, your need to maintain energetic health is even more important since you are highly susceptible to energetic influences. To take control of your intuitive capacities, it is necessary to realize that your needs may be different from your friends or family, regardless of their intuitive sensitivity. And that's okay. Just as your intuitive skills are different than other intuitives, your energetic health needs are different as well.

For example, you may find that you need more quiet time, more time in nature, more space around you, more nutritional emphasis, and so on. At the end of this chapter, I have included an Energy Profile to help you discern your individual needs and preferences according to how intuitive information comes to you. This profile is adapted from the work that I do to help schools and families customize successful environments for highly sensitive children. The more you understand and recognize your own individual energetic needs, the healthier and happier you will be.

No one can take care of your energetic health for you. While energetic practitioners can help you balance and clear your energy field, the daily responsibility of maintaining a strong, clear field is up to you. You wouldn't think of ignoring the importance of brushing your teeth, taking a shower, washing your clothes, or keeping your home clean, so why neglect your energy field? Just as you have a physical body, you have an energy body that encompasses the physical. As we discussed earlier, your healthy energetic body extends about an arm's length in all directions around you.

Just as your physical body can get dirty, perhaps after a day of hiking or strenuous outdoor work, the energetic body can also collect debris. This debris can cause the disturbances (or imbalances) that can eventually show up as mood and behavior challenges, or even physical illness.

Energy Burnout Symptoms

"Energy burnout" is a term that describes when you are overloaded with energetic debris that you may be taking in from a variety of sources, including clients or other people around you, your environment, or even from sources you may not consider such as past traumas, trapped emotions, past lives, or even sources on other energetic planes. For example, if you are a medium who works with people that have crossed over, you can pick up energetic debris as a result. There are a variety of sources of energetic overload, but you don't necessarily need to identify the sources in order to clear your field.

It *is* important for you to identify the signs that you are getting energetically overloaded. Here are just a few:

- Headache
- Nausea
- Dizziness/light-headed
- Out-of-body feeling
- Pressure at the crown of your head
- Mood swings
- Compulsive or addictive behaviors

These are just a few of the indications of energetic overload, and you may have different ones. You may find that you get cravings for certain foods, for example, or you have difficulty concentrating. Over time, you will become aware of how and when other people's energy impacts your mood, behavior, or physical health, and intuitive self-care will become second nature to you.

Self-Care Top Ten

Here are some of the tools that I teach my students and clients to clear energetic debris. Once they start to practice energetic self-care, their lives often change dramatically. We have much more power than we realize to maintain our own health and wellness!

Many of these tools are accessed through intention, focus, and awareness. As I tell my students, the three most important qualities you need to maintain energetic health and develop your intuitive abilities are:

1. Non-judgment (of yourself, others, and your intuitive experiences)
2. Ability to focus (in order to sustain your attention)
3. Willingness to act "as-if" (and take a leap of faith!)

Self-Care Secret #1: Ground!

Have you ever felt "floaty," spacey, or like you weren't quite aligned with what is happening around you? That's a grounding problem and it is extremely common among intuitives. Some intuitives and empaths get so used to the feeling of being ungrounded that they don't realize there is an alternative. As children, some intuitives get in the habit of energetically "escaping" their circumstances, even leaving their physical bodies. But as human beings, we are meant to be grounded in our physical bodies so that we can fully engage in our lives and perform at our best physically, emotionally, mentally, spiritually, and energetically. A grounded intuitive is far more healthy, effective, and reliable than one who is not fully present.

As we mentioned earlier, the best way you can ground yourself is to go out in nature. Nature is always fully present for us and is a great teacher of what it means to be grounded and present. So walk outside in the grass, touch a tree, get out and get some space. Kick off your shoes, go outside, stand barefoot in the grass or sit under a tree. Just five minutes of sunshine can help you get more grounded.

Regular exposure to nature to keep yourself energetically clear is especially important if you are an energy practitioner. The beach is an optimal place for energetic clearing because there is open air (wind is a cleansing force), water from the sea, earth (sand), and metal elements on the ocean floor and in the ocean water. The mountains provide powerful grounding properties as well.

I also use grounding exercises that incorporate the elements of nature. You will see that I don't just use the usual "earth" grounding method, although it is very effective and is the method taught by most healing systems. Once, when I was working with a young boy and I energetically asked him to ground with roots that go into the earth, his energy told me that he didn't want to! He said he didn't want to be stuck in the ground! I asked him how he wanted to ground himself and he showed me a vision of water pouring over him. After that, my practitioner team and I developed grounding methods to work with all the elements. We have found that different clients like different methods, and they can change from day to day, although sometimes we have our favorites.

Remember that you can be creative with these grounding methods and create grounding experiences that work for you.

Grounding with Earth

Close your eyes and imagine a grounding cord shooting down from below your root chakra into the core of the earth, or see roots growing down from your feet to the earth's core. Breathe in Mother Earth's energy from your feet all the way up to your crown chakra. You can also imagine waves of earth energy coming up through your root chakra and centering at your solar plexus area–one wave each for your mind, body, soul, and spirit. You can use the color green to ground and clear your energy with Earth.

Grounding with Air

Close your eyes and inhale deeply, filling your lower abdomen, then chest and shoulder area. Hold your breath at the top. As you exhale, release your breath in a sighing mode. Repeat two more times. Or, stand with your hands over your solar plexus and imagine a breath of air coming through your crown and centering at your solar plexus, using one breath each for your mind, body, soul, and spirit. Another option is to feel a swirl of air moving rapidly around you, like a small cyclone, clearing and grounding your field. You can use the color blue to ground and clear your energy with Earth.

Grounding with Metal

Close your eyes and imagine a large magnet over your head, pulling out unnecessary metals from your body and energy field. Then affirm that your body is drawing up necessary metals from the earth into your body and field. Imagine drawing the metals up from Mother Earth through your feet. You can also imagine waves of whatever metal is necessary for your optimal wellness to come through your root chakra and center at your solar plexus, one each for your mind, body, soul, and spirit. You can use the color silver or grey to ground and clear your energy with Earth.

Grounding with Water

Close your eyes and imagine a spigot over your head. Mentally turn it on and see electric, crystalline water pour through your energy field and body, draining any unwanted energy into Mother Earth to be transmuted into unconditional love. Or, you can imagine a ball of light coming from the spigot through your crown and centering at your solar plexus: one ball of light each for mind, body, soul, and spirit. You can imagine a sparkling clear color to ground and clear your energy with Water.

Grounding with Fire

Touch all five fingertips on both hands together to symbolize a flame. Close your eyes, place your hands over your solar plexus, and imagine fire clearing any blockages there. The flame can also be placed over your head to amplify your connection to the Superconscious mind. Imagine a ball of light coming through the crown and centering at your solar plexus: one ball of flame each for your mind, body, soul, and spirit. Or, you can envision a ring of fire clearing out any debris around your field. You can use the color red to ground and clear your energy with Fire.

There are many ways that you can use nature itself or nature symbols to ground your body. Hiking, walking, taking baths, using hot tubs, saunas or fountains, visualizing rivers and streams, working with salt water, using wind chimes or fans, and bringing fresh air into your space instead of using an air conditioner—all are great methods, just to name a few. Get creative! You can wear various colors to help you ground with the element. (Wearing red to ground with fire, for example.) You can also ground with fire by burning candles or herbs such as sage or Palo Santo, a cleansing herb created from the bark of this special tree.

Final Tip

For a quick grounding method, simply squeeze the fatty pad between your thumb and forefinger with the intention of calling your mind, body, soul, and spirit, back into your body.

Self-Care Secret #2: Meditate

Daily meditation is one of the most useful ways that you can take care of yourself and expand your intuitive abilities at the same time. There are many kinds of meditation for you to try so find one that appeals to your disposition.

Too often, people judge themselves for not being able to meditate and then they quit trying. If sitting meditation is boring to you, try moving meditations such as walking or tai chi. The point is for you to practice focused awareness and train your mind. Any way that you can work on mindfulness is good. Just practicing being fully present and mindful, even when doing something as simple as washing dishes is helpful!

Self-Care Secret #3: Nourish Yourself and Detox

As your intuitive abilities develop and your vibrational frequency increases, you will want to make sure your physical body is healthy enough to sustain your higher vibration. This means that nourishing yourself with healthy food and plenty of clean water is extremely important. Often, people find that as they learn to manage their intuitive abilities, they have an impulse to improve their diet or make other healthy lifestyle changes.

Several years ago, I began to co-facilitate a 40-day nutrition, fasting, and detoxification program. This program has brought me a tremendous amount of mental clarity, sharpened my intuition, and helped me lose twenty-five pounds. At one point after finishing the 40-day program, I remember feeling like I was floating on a cloud and experiencing pure bliss. It was so astounding that I wondered if that feeling is what is meant in the Bible when they refer to a "peace that surpasses all understanding."

Healthy nutrition is vital for intuitives, empaths, and highly sensitive people. Find a program that works for you—and don't forget to include detoxification methods into your lifestyle. We often don't realize how important detoxifying is to maintain balance and wellness. It is something most people don't do enough and intuitive people need to do it even more than others. Like nutrition, your methods of detoxification will depend on what works for your individual body and temperament. Liver cleanses are especially important to keep your body and energy field detoxified. I advise my students to engage in liver cleansing at least twice a year.

Some detox methods that can help you keep your body and energy field clear are various forms of short-term fasting, juice cleanses, supplements that cleanse, saunas and hot springs, colonics, and hydrotherapy. These are *not* just beauty or "luxury" experiences. I have learned that detoxification is an essential part of maintaining good health. So check into local spas and wellness centers and make them a regular part of your health and energy care practice.

Self-Care Secret #4: Get Enough Trace Minerals

Most highly sensitive people are low on trace minerals because the energy body burns trace minerals for fuel, including magnesium, zinc, copper, selenium, and iodine in the same way that the physical body burns carbohydrates. Intuitive people are low on these minerals because they burn through them.

Trace minerals are also commonly lacking in many people because our soil and water have been stripped of trace minerals. As an intuitive, you need to pay special attention to make sure your trace minerals are high and balanced.

Here are several ways you can maintain healthy trace mineral levels:

- See your holistic healthcare practitioner to have your trace mineral levels tested, or check at your local health food store for trace mineral supplements you can add to your water. Trace Minerals Research Concentrate® is a brand I have used with success.

- Take a bath with Epsom salts in the water. Trace minerals can be absorbed through the skin, so make sure there are no artificial chemicals or fragrances added to the salts. The magnesium will also help you relax your muscles, sleep better, and restore your energy field.

- Footbaths with Epsom salts also allow for transdermal absorption.

- You can make your own magnesium oil to use on your body. (Check online for recipes.)

- You can put magnesium oil on the bottom of your feet before you put your socks on. This method can also be used with children. You can mix magnesium oil with coconut oil as well.

Note: Monitor the magnesium dosage you use. Too much magnesium can result in diarrhea. If this happens, health care practitioners recommend that you decrease the dosage.

Self-Care Secret #5: Eat Foods to Support Serotonin and Dopamine Levels

I tend to have cravings for chocolate after energy trainings or in between client sessions. I've also noticed that some form of chocolate (mostly commercial grade) is usually offered during breaks at many of the energy trainings I have attended over the years. It took a while for me to make the connection between chocolate cravings and the need to balance neurotransmitters in the brain while doing intuitive work.

Cacao, the bean used to make chocolate, is well known as a "feel good food" and may increase levels of serotonin and endorphins in the brain. Anandamide, often referred to as the bliss chemical, has also been identified in raw cacao. Raw cacao is high in magnesium and other trace minerals that support serotonin production and balance the nervous system. It is very important for people who do intuitive work to maintain a good balance of these neurotransmitters as they are directly related to sleep, mood, memory and learning.

The following recipe is one that I now use and recommend in place of commercial chocolates that have high levels of refined sugars and dairy milk. One of my child clients enjoys this beverage in place of regular hot chocolate or chocolate bars. She lovingly refers to it as Chocolate Medicine, so that's what we named the recipe.

Chocolate Medicine
¼ cup of organic raw cacao powder
1 cup of almond milk (or other non-dairy milk alternative)
1 cup of water
¼ tsp of cinnamon
¼ tsp of nutmeg
1 tbsp of vanilla extract
2 tbsp of raw local organic honey

Heat (but do not boil) water and almond milk. Add all remaining ingredients and stir until the mixture is smooth. Allow mixture to simmer for approximately 10 minutes on low heat. Remove from stove and add honey to taste. Add more almond milk or water to make a thinner consistency.

I also recommend that you consult nutrition guides to find lists of foods that are known to support healthy levels of serotonin and dopamine. Consider making these foods a part of your regular diet, especially if you plan to actively learn to work with energy and intuition.

Self-Care Secret #6: Clear Your Environment

Your home environment is very important to maintaining a clear, healthy energy field. This is especially true for intuitive people. Take some time to sense the energy in each room of your home. What do you feel or see? What is needed to clear the energy? What needs to be added to help you feel clear and calm, or what needs to be taken away, such as clutter?

Here are a few steps you can take to clear the energy at home and at work:

- Research electromagnetic frequencies and consider using devices that can help block any damage they might do. (Consider devices to protect you from cell phone radiation as well.)
- Consider use of essential oils in diffusers. Find the ones that work best for you
- Use stones or crystals to help clear your home or work
- Sage, Palo Santo, and other herbs can be used for energy cleansing
- Himalayan salt lamps or bowls of Himalayan salt can help to keep energy clear.
- Research space or room energy clearing methods. A simple one is to envision negative energy spiraling into the center of the room and flushing away.
- Ask your spirit guides, angels, etc. to help keep your space clear.

- Regularly clean everything, especially anything that is touched by other people, such as door handles and light switches.

- You can use sound to clear the energy in your room, with singing or instruments such as gongs, Tibetan bowls, drums, or rattles.

There are many more methods. Find what works for you. Also keep in mind that if you do energy work in your home, a great deal of energy is being cleared and it becomes especially important to maintain good energy hygiene. Some practitioners choose not to work in their home space in order to keep their home environment clear. (See "Special Notes for Energy Practitioners" below.)

Special Notes for Energy Practitioners

If you are an energy practitioner, such as an energy therapist, Reiki master, or shaman, you will need to take extra steps to keep you and your environment clear of energetic debris. Here are a few tips:

- Have regular energy sessions for yourself performed by another practitioner. This helps keep your field clear. Perhaps plan trades with other energy practitioners.

- Wash your hands after working with each client.

- Shower daily to clear energy sessions. Take your shower in the evening rather than the next morning, if possible.

- Wash all clothes worn during sessions. Use wash-and-wear clothing that does not require dry cleaning.
- Maintain proper boundaries when working with a client. For the Innerlight Method, I remain outside the client's energy field and do not enter into it. However, if you use a method where you enter into a client's field, make sure that you consciously leave their field after the session.
- Always consciously close your energy field after each session.
- Drink a lot of water.
- Use Emergen-C® to balance electrolytes that are used as fuel when you do energy work.

Self-Care Secret #7: Tune In to Your Energy Regularly

On an intuitive level, tune in to determine the circumstances, time of day, or people (this may be as simple as the number of people around you or the noise volume) that seem to cause you to become energetically overloaded. Recognize the patterns that emerge and take any steps you can to either remind yourself to do energy clearing exercises, or to avoid being in these situations for extended periods of time.

Self-Care Secret #8: Shield Your Energy When Needed

Practice energy shielding when needed. You can also teach your children to practice energy shielding as well. For example, before you leave the house each morning, visualize yourself and your child being enclosed in a ball of golden light. Say a prayer (or set an intention) that the ball of light be filled with the energy of pure, unconditional love. Affirm that only the energy of love may pass through your energetic boundary. Remind yourself that this is done in the spirit of preparation and not with any intention to be overly defensive or overprotective. Set an intention for all good energy to come to you.

Self-Care Secret #9: Exercise Your Field

In our Innerlight Method training, we use exercises that were chosen with the intention of clearing energetic blending, expanding and strengthening the energy field, balancing the endocrine system, and cutting unhealthy energetic ties to others. Remember that when we take on energy from around us, it typically enters the body and nervous system through the solar plexus. This can create stomach problems such as stomach aches and constipation.

Exercises that help expand your field focus on having your arms or legs extended away from your body. Exercises that cut energetic cords are those that cross the midline of the body. These exercises are also beneficial for balancing the left and right hemispheres of the brain.

All of the exercises below are ones that I learned from my yoga practice, and have helped me to release empathic overload. I owe a great debt of gratitude to my Kundalini Yoga teachers for helping me develop these life-sustaining skills. You should be aware that these exercises generate a very powerful movement of energy. Please consult your health care professional before practicing these exercises, especially if you have heart issues.

Spinal Twist Exercise

Sit in a comfortable cross-legged position. Place your hands on your shoulders—right hand on right shoulder, left hand on left shoulder—with your fingers in front and the thumbs in back. Begin twisting from side to side, inhaling as you twist left and exhaling as you twist right. Your arms should remain parallel with the ground. Your head remains still and moves as a natural extension of your spine. Continue for one minute. This exercise wrings out the solar plexus like a washing machine on the spin cycle, and clears any excess energy that does not belong to you. The movement of the arms also expands your energy field.

Leg Scissor Exercise

Sit with your legs extended straight in front of you. Place your hands on the floor behind your hips and about a hands length behind your body. Lean back onto your hands or forearms. Lift your legs and begin scissoring them in front of your body. Inhale powerfully as you open your legs wide apart, and exhale powerfully as you draw your legs together and cross them. Repeat for 1-2 minutes. This exercise helps to cut any energetic cords to other people and clears and expands your field.

Push/Pull Exercise

Sit with your legs extended out straight in front of you. Place your hands behind your hips, about a single hands-length behind your body. Lean back onto your hands or forearms. Keeping your legs together, inhale as you bring your legs in toward your chest, and exhale as you push your legs out and upward. Repeat for 1-2 minutes. This exercise pushes unwanted energy out of your energetic field and expands your field.

Cross Crawl Exercise

Stand up straight with your legs hip-width apart. Extend your arms out sixty degrees from your body. Begin marching in place. As your left knee comes up, extend your right hand or elbow to tap the knee. As your right knee comes up, extend your left hand or elbow to tap the knee. Repeat for 1-2 minutes. This exercise helps to synchronize the left and right hemispheres of the brain, bringing the intuitive and the intellectual into balance.

Arm Circle Exercise

Stand with your feet hip-width apart. Begin circling your arms in one direction. Make big circles for 1 minute. Change directions and continue making circles with your arms for another minute. This exercise clears and expands your energy field.

Self-Care Secret #10: Honor Your Energetic Needs

When I work with intuitive families, it is common for each family member to have different energetic needs. One child may be at their best early in the morning while the parents are most productive late at night. One child needs a lot of stimulation and variety in their environment while another needs a quiet, restful place. One parent likes bright lights and loud concerts and the other parent is overwhelmed by them. Often we don't realize what is making us agitated, anxious, or unhappy—and simple changes in our environment or daily schedule can solve the problem.

Choices you make every day for yourself or for your children can either make a net deposit or withdrawal from your "energetic bank account." For example, if you need a lot of light, putting your home office in the basement is unlikely to work well. If your child is sensitive to too much light, studying in a brightly lit kitchen will not work well either.

The same thing happens in classrooms. Every child has different needs in order to learn and perform at their best. This is true with most children, but intuitive and highly sensitive children have even greater differences in what they need in order to shine their unique genius.

I work with schools and families to help identify energetic needs and create plans that can benefit the whole family or classroom without leaving anyone out. The first step in the process is to identify the unique individual needs. The

Energy Profile in the next section can help you understand how you can design your life to be your energetic best.

The Energy Profile is a tool to get you started on identifying your energetic needs and creating new, conscious strategies for greater health, success, and happiness.

Embrace Your Energy Profile

There are no right or wrong answers and no grades at the end! The idea is for you to think about what works and doesn't work for you, so that you can bring greater awareness to how you plan your day and your life.

INTUITIVE STYLE PROFILE

Directions: Place a check mark next to all answers that apply. This will give you more insight into how intuitive information comes to you. Once you've checked each statement that rings true for you, you may want to then identify each statement according to the primary intuitive pathway it demonstrates—that way, you can tally your responses and have a better picture of which pathway is most likely your primary pathway. (For example, the first statement would get a "K" for Kinesthetic Intuitive. If you're not sure of the intuitive type characteristics, you can review the Intuitive Types and Intuitive Pathways described in chapter 2.)

_____ I can enter a room for the first time and feel the energy of what happened there in the past.

_____ I often have dreams that I remember in vivid detail. They often come true.

_____ I'm able to draw or create designs from images I see in my mind's eye.

_____ I can literally hear what others are thinking.

_____ I suddenly get amazing ideas and don't know where they came from.

_____ I know who's calling before I answer the phone.

_____ Sometimes I just know things about a person before they ever speak to me.

_____ I can taste a dish and automatically know all the ingredients and spices in it.

_____ I can see or hear people who others can't see or hear.

_____ I communicate with angels and often receive messages that guide me or others.

_____ I see auras or colors around people's bodies.

_____ I know the answer to complex math problems without calculating all the steps.

_____ I can sometimes see myself as if I am floating above my body.

_____ I experience frequent unexplained stomachaches or pains when I enter crowded places.

_____ I am able to actually taste a substance without putting it in my mouth.

_____ When someone is sad or hurt, I can feel their pain or their feelings in my body.

_____ I can hear a voice inside my mind that helps me write stories, make music, or know what to say.

_____ I can sometimes pick up on smells/scents that are not present in the room.

_____ I have been told that I help people heal physical ailments by touching them.

_____ Since I was young, people close to me have complained that I am "too sensitive."

Final Notes: Did anything surprise you about your answers? Remember that the purpose of this profile is simply to help you understand yourself and your intuition better. If you checked more than ten of these statements, it is likely that your intuitive abilities are exceptionally high and multi-sensory. Consistent self-care is an important consideration for you to continue to develop your capacity while maintaining excellent physical, mental, and emotional health.

ENERGY PROFILE

Directions: The following energy profile will help you explore the impact your environment has on your energetic wellbeing as an empathic or intuitive person.

This section helps you understand how you respond energetically to color, lights, sound, scents, and interactions with people. Please answer each of the following questions according to how you usually feel.

A. Social Engagement

_____ I typically prefer to be alone.

_____ I typically prefer to socialize with other people.

_____ I am most productive when working alone.

_____ I am most productive and energized when working with others.

Do you like to work in groups? Check all of the social group sizes in which you feel comfortable and most energized.

_____ Small group: 1-3 people

_____ Medium group: 4-10 people

_____ Medium/Large group: 11-29 people

_____ Large groups: 30 or more people

_____ I enjoy hugging, touching, or holding hands with others.

_____ I feel anxious when others attempt to hug or touch me.

_____ I feel very comfortable when I am in close physical proximity with others.

_____ I feel uncomfortable when people stand too close to me.

_____ I seek out and enjoy social interactions with close friends.

_____ It bothers me when someone is talking non-stop.

I prefer to:

_____ Talk continuously

_____ Be quiet most of the time

_____ Talk only when I have something to say

B. Work Style

_____ I work best when my environment is quiet.

_____ I am able to ignore the noise of other people talking while I am working.

_____ I will work on an assignment until it is completed, no matter what.

_____ When I receive an assignment, I need to have exact steps on how to complete it. I prefer to have unlimited amount of time to work on an assignment.

_____ I need to have clear deadlines in order to complete an assignment.

_____ I get more work done when I am alone.

_____ I like to do things spontaneously.

_____ I like to do things on schedule.

_____ I motivate myself to work hard.

_____ I am motivated to do my best to earn approval or recognition from others.

_____ I enjoy participating in group discussions.

_____ I would rather work with a team to complete important projects.

_____ If I have to decide something, I ask the group for opinions.

_____ I can read the energy of a group and make choices that support what everyone in the group needs.

C. Body Rhythms

Write the time of day (e.g. 8am-10am) when you feel most energized and able to focus on the following important tasks:

_____ Learning a new concept

_____ Exercising

_____ Holding important conversations

_____ Completing challenging work assignments

_____ Thinking creatively

_____ Meditating or praying

Write the time of day (e.g. 8am-10am) when you feel least energized and unable to focus on the following important tasks:

_____ Learning a new concept

_____ Exercising

_____ Holding important conversations

_____ Completing challenging work assignments

_____ Thinking creatively

_____ Meditating or praying

_____ My body requires frequent breaks in order to sustain concentration over a long period of time.

_____ It is easy for me to sustain focused concentration for long periods of time.

_____ If I have to sit still for a long time, I need to tap, shake my leg, or move my body in some way.

I concentrate best:

_____ sitting at a desk or table.

_____ stretched out on my bed.

_____ while exercising or engaging in a physical activity.

_____ sitting outdoors in nature.

_____ at a coffee shop, library, or other public setting.

D. Nature Therapy

_____ I crave being outdoors in nature and make time to enjoy it.

_____ I like being outdoors in nature but rarely make time to do it.

_____ I typically avoid outdoor activities.

Which of the following natural environments do you find most restorative and energizing:

_____ Desert	_____ Mountain	_____ Lake
_____ City Park	_____ Ocean	_____ Forest
_____ Farm	_____ Meadow/Pasture	_____ Garden

In what way does being in these environments support you?

_____

_____

Which of the following natural environments do you tend to avoid:

_____ Desert _____ Mountain _____ Lake

_____ City Park _____ Ocean _____ Forest

_____ Farm _____ Meadow/Pasture _____ Garden

In what way does being in these environments negatively impact your mood or sense of wellbeing?

_____

_____

_____ I can work productively in an enclosed, small space with no windows.

_____ I need open space and windows in order to work productively.

_____ I can work productively in a cluttered or disorganized space.

_____ I work best in an organized and clutter-free work space.

E. Color Therapy

What is your favorite color?

_____

Which colors are you drawn to that help you feel calm and relaxed?

_____

Which colors are you drawn to that help you focus and concentrate?

_____

What colors make you feel inspired?

_____

What colors make you feel uptight or claustrophobic?

_____

What color would you never wear?

—_____

If you could paint your room, what color would you paint it?

_____

If you could wear any color clothes, what color would you wear most? Why?

_____

F. Light Therapy

Do you prefer a room with or without windows? Why?

_____

Describe your need for natural sunlight.

_____

Describe how fluorescent lights affect you. Do they bother you or give you a headache?

_____

G. Sound Therapy

Describe the importance of music and sound in your life.

_____

Describe how your productivity is affected when you work with music playing in the background?

_____

What type of music relaxes you?

_____

What type of music is helpful to keep you productive?

_____

What type of music agitates you or do you actively avoid?

_____

What sounds of nature do you find soothing and healing?

_____

Explain your sensitivity to loud sounds in the environment or in crowds. How does it affect you?

_____

H. Aromatherapy

What smells make you feel calm and relaxed?

_____

What kinds of smells do you like?

_____

What smells do you find repulsive or actively avoid?

_____

How important is it for you or your environment to smell good?

_____

Describe how you feel when a person near you is wearing perfume?

_____

Which household chemical smells make you feel sick or give you a headache?

_____

I. Temperature

Describe your need for fresh air.

Describe any physical or mood changes you may experience when you have been in an air conditioned building for an extended period of time.

_____

Explain how you feel when you are in an environment that is too cold.

_____

Explain how you feel when you are in an environment that is too hot.

_____

Describe how your energy or concentration is affected when you work in a stuffy environment.

_____

J. Physical Nourishment

List three foods that make you feel energized and clear-minded after you eat them.

_____

List three foods that make you feel tired or leave your brain feeling foggy after eating them.

_____

Name the type of food you tend to eat when you feel upset.

_____

Name the top three foods that you crave and cannot live without.

_____

How frequently do you need to eat in order to maintain your energy levels throughout the day?

_____

Final Notes: What did you learn from answering these questions? Take a little time to write down any thoughts you have about your answers, and also any ideas for how you can adapt your schedule, your environment, your work, or your life to better meet the energetic needs you have identified. Please remember that the more you operate within your natural energy profile, the more energy and vitality you will have to face the world and to maintain healthy energetic boundaries.

Now You Can Integrate

With all of these tools and practices, you'll find yourself becoming more and more able to access and utilize your gifts without becoming overwhelmed. The next step is being able to combine your intuition and intellect into the integrated force of genius they're meant to be. It's time to learn about this integration process and see how it can change your life and help you change the world!

7

Step Seven: Balance Your Intuition and Intellect

Integrating Your Genius

"Niki, we love what you've been doing with the students here at school. The staff and parents have noticed the transformation that has taken place with many of the children you served." The director paused before continuing. "But I am really concerned about my responsibility to uphold the separation of church and state. I know you've explained that energy work is not religious, but we are worried that some parents feel that we are promoting a religious experience. I need to ask you not to practice energy balancing here on campus again until I understand more about it."

Oh my goodness. No more working with the children here? Then how will I be able to help them?

The truth is that when my intuitive faculties broke open, I found myself totally immersed in this right-brained world of intuition and energy. I became completely fascinated with this meditative, spiritual side of life and with helping other people. I loved it. As with many intuitives, the time came when I wondered if I should quit my job and use my intuitive skills to make a living. Some people feel that if you have intuitive gifts, you're "supposed" to become a full-time psychic, medium, or healer. Yet I knew people who had done just that, but had not been able to succeed at making a living. I figured that it might be in my future, but in the meantime, I was supporting the growth of a charter school and loving my work with the children.

Now that the charter school was asking me not to practice energy work on campus, I was not only looking at the prospect of quitting my job to start a full-time energy balancing practice, but I came face-to-face with some serious questions. Why had I spent most of my life working so diligently at my career in education, only to be spiritually led in this new direction of intuition and energy? I helped build and launch charter schools, had a bachelor's degree from Berkeley, a master's degree from Columbia, and a PhD from UCLA. Why had I spent all those years getting an education if I was planning to walk away from it to pursue a completely different field? Especially one that is not well accepted or respected by my academic peers?

All that work in the logical, academic realm seemed to be as earthbound and left-brained as it gets. So, why was I now in this new world of energy medicine that seemed far removed from that world?

I asked Spirit, "Why in the world did you make me waste all those years getting that expensive education just to send me into the complete opposite direction?"

Bringing It All Together

The answer I received was to look at things differently. Does it really need to be one world or the other? Does it have to be logic and intuition pitted against each other, with one side stereotyped as narrow-minded and the other typecast as neurotic? Do we need to judge or choose between them? I saw that I needed to merge and balance the two sides— left- and right-brain, masculine and feminine, intellect and intuition. I had to marry my linear, "prove-it-to-me" side with my intuitive, experiential side. It wasn't that one side was better than the other, but rather that I needed to integrate them. In meditation I heard the question, "What would it be like if the intuitive gifts were meant to be funneled through your background of education? What would the merger of your intuitive gifts and your passion for education look like?"

I thought about William. His mother brought him to see me because school and health care professionals thought he should begin taking medication for anxiety problems. He was having terrible panic attacks and nothing else was working. I did three energy balancing sessions with him and his panic attacks and meltdowns stopped completely. The doctors cancelled the prescription for medication. (Note: This isn't to say that energy balancing is a substitute for medication, because medication is often helpful and necessary. But it doesn't need to be the first resort—there are other options to try. I have worked with many children like William whose challenges could be addressed partially or completely with the Innerlight Method.)

I could see that I was not meant to disconnect from what I did before. Instead, I was meant to bring intuition and energy healing into education and child development to create something unique that the world needed. I left the charter school I had founded and began a full-time energy balancing practice focused on children. I quickly noticed that intuitive children have intuitive parents, and they often wanted help too. In fact, whole families came for help. Then educators, health care professionals, ministers, and other people started to call. While I expanded my practice to help these additional people, I continued to focus on the needs of gifted children. I began to see that by merging my academic background with my energy gifts, I could help create a new way of approaching education. So I went back to Aveson, the charter school I had once worked at, and introduced energy balancing into the school setting.

At Aveson, I trained Shay, a very gifted teacher and intuitive, to use Innerlight Method techniques (with parental permission and staff supervision) in her classroom for highly sensitive children in first through fifth grades. These were children who were frequently being sent out of their classrooms for behavior problems, often requiring intervention and medication. The project was highly successful. After the Innerlight Method was implemented, the classroom had a zero referral rate, meaning not one child was sent out of the room for behavior problems. By merging intellect and intuition, I could help change how people approached educating, raising, and treating highly sensitive children!

This was only the beginning.

Shay and I created an independent study program with an individualized, self-paced course of study that included passion projects so all the children could dive deeply into subject matter of deep interest to them. The program was highly successful and in great demand from parents who wanted their children in the program. Then the founder and co-director of a local preschool took the Innerlight Method training and recommended that we perform energy balancing at the school for parents and teachers. From there, the school asked that we help them incorporate energy balancing principles into how they set up their classrooms. This was very exciting! Educators were beginning to integrate energy balancing principles into the very structure, design, and management of the school. This became my vision: to make energy awareness part of our mainstream approach to education.

Coming Up Out of the Rabbit Hole

It's hard to believe my healing journey all started with feeling other people's pains in my body. As I opened up to my intuitive empathy and learned how to manage it, I realized I wanted to help other people come up out of the intuitive "rabbit hole" and create balance for themselves and others. An exciting new future opened up for me when I realized I could help children (and eventually adults) come out of isolation and fear to bring their unique genius into the light of day—and make a positive difference in the world.

Working with intuitive children, it's hard *not* to see the great potential they have to share their gifts to help the planet. Rather than putting these gifts aside, we can integrate them into everyday life to create an exciting future. Who knows what problems we might solve when we are working at our full intellectual *and* intuitive capacity?

Expanding the Vision

The dream continues to grow. Shay is now developing a private school that will totally merge energy principles into the setting and curriculum, as she builds the school from the ground up.

We have presented the Innerlight Method at the college level to help students prepare for final exams and made it part of their parent education program. We are also making inroads into healthcare and have presented it to social work professionals at Kaiser Permanente.

I now understand why I was first guided to academic study and then to intuitive work. Having a solid academic background helped establish my credibility, so that people in medical and academic environments would listen to me. It has opened doors within settings where intuition and energy awareness can bring tremendous benefit.

By merging my background and passion with my intuitive gifts, I am able to serve as a bridge between logic and intuition, so these worlds can live side by side. I can create new opportunities for gifted and highly sensitive children, and shift how educators and health care professionals view intuitive children and adults differently, so they can be supported in making their genius-level contributions to society.

What Does Your Genius Look Like?

So you've accepted, identified, and taken charge of your abilities, and you're learning to use your gifts without feeling other people's pain. You know how to clear your energy, take care of yourself, and find the right kind of support. Congratulations! You're well on your way to developing your abilities without absorbing other people's energy. Now what?

When you wonder if your intuitive gifts are going to take you far away from life as you know it, remember that nothing has to be thrown away in order to use your talents. Sometimes it is in our path to move on, let go of relationships, change jobs, or start a new business, but that is up to us to decide (ideally with the help of intuitive peers and mentors). You don't have to go to the mountaintop and stay there! You can take the mountaintop experiences back into your everyday life, to your family and friends, and into your work and community.

What does it look like for you when your intuitive gifts live inside the life you have already developed for yourself? What is your inner voice of wisdom calling for you to create?

Among my students and clients, there are so many examples of creative ways to apply intuition. As mentioned earlier, my student and co-worker, Shay, went from a first-time teacher who trained in energy balancing, to become a consultant for teachers and parents, and is now using the principles of energy balancing to create her own school. She is an example of a student whose abilities quickly equaled the teacher's!

I have trained hypnotherapists, social workers, and mental health therapists to bring the Innerlight Method principles into their practices. Imagine a future where therapists utilize their intuitive experience, recognize the impact of energy overload, and are able to treat it with energy balancing, just as they treat mental health conditions! One of my therapist students tells me that her clients who choose to do energy balancing along with their regular therapy recover much more quickly than those who don't.

I have trained teachers who can bring energy principles into schools, and many parents who can re-structure their life at home based on nurturing every family member's energetic needs. I have students who apply the Innerlight Method to help animals. I have a student who is an architect who uses her intuition to read the energy of land or to better understand the intuitive needs of her clients. Just think if our buildings were designed intuitively with a goal of supporting us energetically, rather than overloading or depleting us! What would that workplace or hospital look like?

One of my students is a writer and poet. She can use her gifts to intuit the needs or voices of the clients she writes for, and to open up her creative channel for poetry. She is a trained Innerlight Method practitioner and uses energy balancing to help other writers and artists open up their creative channels. She also studies shamanism and combines energy balancing with shamanic arts to help intuitive adults clear spiritual blockages.

The opportunities to integrate intuition into our daily lives are endless. Think of the discoveries that can be made by intuitive scientists, the breakthroughs that could come from intuitive engineers, or the healing that could be achieved by intuitive doctors! What kind of surgeon could you be if you could feel what's happening with the health of your patients?

Best of all, these accomplishments can be made by thriving individuals who are physically healthy and expanded energetically, with solid energetic boundaries so they aren't absorbing the feelings of others. Their services are likely to be in high demand because they can bring a level of awareness and invention that others can't into their clients' lives.

We can hold ourselves back because we assume in advance that our credibility or even our sanity will be questioned. Early in my career, I spent so much time thinking that I would be rejected or ridiculed, but the truth is that I have never met a hostile audience.

In every organization I have encountered, at least a third of the participants had some of the symptoms I have described in this book. They could relate to being intuitive, empathic, or highly sensitive. I promise you that in any environment you find yourself in, no matter how conventional, there will be people who have had your experiences, and they are waiting for you to open up the conversation.

A Vision for Tomorrow

You woke up this morning, brushed your teeth, and balanced your energy field. It has become one more thing you automatically do because it is part of who you are. You no longer see your intuition as something big and scary. Instead, it is a part of your life that you are matter-of-fact about when talking or interacting with others. Managing it is part of your daily routine to stay in optimal health and balance.

I believe we are rapidly moving to a time when intuitive gifts are everyday occurrences that we manage on a daily basis. We are increasingly recognizing that intuitive gifts are part of the human range of ability that we all share to varying degrees. We are beginning to understand the importance of activating the unique gifts that are in each of us, and using these gifts to improve how we manage our families, deliver education and healthcare, and structure our society.

In the larger sense, when we squash and suppress our awareness, we give away our power to co-create with the higher wisdom that we all access. How differently would people react to threats such as terrorism and climate change if they were able to directly access higher wisdom to find solutions rather than react with worry, fear, rage, or indifference?

As more people wake up to their intuitive faculties and learn to use these gifts without being overloaded by them, we will enjoy the benefits of their genius level contributions across all aspects of society.

I can't help but think about how exciting it will be when everyone feels fully connected to his or her inner wisdom, without apology, and without fear. When people are comfortable and open with their intuition, we will be able to synchronistically come together for the greater good as we all access higher wisdom and the truth. I believe the answers to our greatest challenges, our next amazing inventions, and the solutions to achieve freedom and peace are just waiting for us to access them in the intuitive realm. It's time for intuition and energy awareness to become part of our mainstream conversation.

Your Fearless Future

People think of Einstein as a genius, but he acknowledged that his intuition was more relevant than his knowledge. In fact, he said he dreamed his famous theory of relativity! Imagine if he had ignored his intuition instead of applying it to his field of passion?

How are you going to integrate *your* gifts with discernment, boundaries, and a sense of purpose to help your life and your community? How are you going to assimilate your logical and mystical sides, the masculine and feminine, the material and the spiritual, so that it exists harmoniously inside of you and works in service of your passions and talents? We each have unique, individual gifts, and when we embrace them no one can compete with what we have to offer. You were not meant to stand alone or hide in the dark, but to work with humanity. When you learn to let go of everything that has caused you to fear your gifts, and begin to see how your gifts are fitted to your destiny, you become unstoppable.

I hope you will find the courage to take responsibility for your energetic well-being and say yes to the total expression of your intuitive gifts. You don't have to suppress them or become overwhelmed by them. Your gifts don't have to separate you from the world. They can help you engage more fully and contribute in ways you may not be able to imagine…yet!

If you are considering ignoring or minimizing your gifts, the real question might be, *What gifts are you leaving behind because you are afraid to align with your inner wisdom?* You owe it to yourself and the world to explore all of who you are, and pursue the genius contributions only you can make. You came to this planet to fulfill a mission by embracing the totality of who you are, including your unique energetic signature and the full use of your intuitive senses.

Your gifts were given to you for a purpose. Embrace them with fearless passion! May you enjoy your journey of expanding and growing into your highest potential.

Three Exercises to Integrate Your Intuition

Exercise #1- Intuitive Grocer Exercise

It's time to develop your intuition! Similar to learning anything new (such as a new topic, sport, or hobby), there is a natural learning curve to sharpening your intuition. When you set the intention to notice your natural intuition that already exists, you will begin to strengthen your intuitive muscles.

Intuition can be used in your daily life in many ways. The next time you're at the grocery store, practice the following "Intuitive Grocer" assignment. Follow the steps below to complete this activity.

Step 1: "Test" different foods and brands by asking for intuitive information. Pick up the type of food or brand you usually buy, and then select a different food or brand. What information are you receiving?

Step 2: Listen to your intuition. Is one type of food or brand better for you and your family?

Step 3: Observe, journal, and record what you notice. Are there positive changes in the health and energy of your family as you begin to grocery shop intuitively? How does your life shift when you lean into and trust your intuition?

(Note: The act of writing and journaling is proven to help connect people to their intuitive senses.)

Exercise #2- Meditative Q&A Exercise

Intuition can be used to deliver and retrieve important information. Follow these steps to complete this exercise:

Step 1: Find a quiet place, take a few deep breaths, and focus your attention into the center of your mind.

Step 2: Relax and allow yourself to drop into a deeper state of meditation.

Step 3: Next, ask yourself a question and wait for the response.

Step 4: Record your reply and how you received it. Did you see, hear, or sense it? Was it easy for you to receive information? Did you trust the information you received or did you find yourself second-guessing the reply? Did you receive a reply through intuitive observation, intuitive conversation, or in another way?

Exercise #3- Plan Your Genius Exercise

How are you going to integrate your intellect and your intuition to express your true genius? Answer these questions to begin crafting your vision.

1. I would like to explore or study these intuitive areas or fields:

   _____

   _____

   _____

   _____

2. My intuitive gifts or strengths include:

   _____

   _____

   _____

   _____

3. My current or professional career interests are:

   _____

   _____

   _____

   _____

4. Some creative ways that I could blend my current interests with my intuitive gifts in my personal life (relationships, finance, health, spirituality, hobbies, etc.) are:

_____

_____

_____

_____

5. How am I being invited to merge my professional background, passions, or interests with my intuitive gifts?

_____

_____

_____

_____

6. My "big" vision (think big and include any plans for intuitive careers or business ideas, and any other plans or dreams you have related to your intuition) for my intuitive future is:

_____

_____

_____

_____

7. My inner wisdom (or spiritual guidance) is giving me these messages about who I am as an intuitive being and how to best express my intuitive abilities:

_____

_____

_____

_____

Taking Action

If you've been taking action as you've been reading this book, you know that action is where true healing and transformation happens. I encourage you to continue using all of the tools and practices you've learned here and watch the results compound over time. If you find yourself feeling a little stuck or overwhelmed, it may mean that your soul is taking you to a new level of expansion of your gifts. When you find that happening, go back to the beginning of the book and work the seven-step system again. If you find yourself needing more support, I recommend that you reach out to your community—and stay in the flow.

Conclusion

I Feel Your Possibility

S ince you made it to the end of this book, you surely realize that this 7-Step Survival Guide was actually intended to help you do much more than just *survive* as an empathic person. The truest intention behind this book is to offer you an invitation to *thrive* as an intuitive and empathic person who brings 100 percent of your gifts and talents into full expression in every area of your life. I hope you will take this invitation to heart by incorporating the tips and techniques offered here in your daily energy hygiene routine. Energetic self-care and boundary work are lifelong habits that need to be practiced as regularly as brushing your teeth or combing your hair. Our energetic boundaries and intuitive receptivity are in a state of continuous flux depending on our current state of health, emotional wellbeing, life stress, and relationship dynamics. A healthy and balanced use of our intuitive abilities is something that must constantly be renegotiated and realigned as we evolve spiritually, emotionally, and physically. The worst thing we can do is to consider these techniques to be a one-time fix for our struggles.

As you continue with this journey, you may begin to notice the quiet nudging of your inner intuitive guidance asking you to make other changes in your life that will support your development and continue to expand your intuition. Over time, you may find yourself being intuitively guided to change your choice of entertainment away from violent or aggressive content toward music, film, and television programs that are more uplifting and encouraging. You may find your intuition guiding you away from eating fast food toward a more healthy and natural diet. Some people find their social circles evolve toward people who are more positive and optimistic.

All of these changes will make it possible for your nervous system to handle greater amounts of intuitive energy and information over time. This evolution will look different for each person. It will be important to take time to be gentle with yourself since an accelerated pace of personal expansion may cause you to feel as if your whole worldview is changing overnight. Remember to move at a pace that feels good for you, but I encourage you to resist the urge to return to your former habits.

If you take this invitation to heart, you will find it increasingly easier to set healthy energetic boundaries and use your intuitive gifts to navigate your world. Over time, you will begin to experience a greater sense of flow and synchronicity—almost as if some of life's problems begin to solve themselves with a fraction of the effort you expended in the past. You may also notice significant shifts in personal and professional relationships, especially those where your lack of energetic boundaries caused you to overextend yourself in unhealthy ways. It may take time for your loved ones and co-workers to adjust to the new you, but I promise you will never look back to the old days when you felt responsible for feeling everyone else's pain!

Please remember, this journey is easier with other like-minded, like-gifted people. It's not a path that's meant to be walked alone. We are all connected at our core for a reason, and we can help each other soar to new heights.

Thank you for inviting me to be a part of your soul's journey by picking up this book. My prayer is that you will use what you've learned here to feel less of other people's pain and more of your own possibility!

About Innerlight
Method Sessions

Receiving an Energy Balancing Session

Receiving energy balancing or energy therapy for yourself can be extremely useful for keeping your energy clear and developing your intuitive skills. There are many different schools of energy healing, including color therapy, sound and music therapy, light therapy, aromatherapy, nutritional healing, homeopathy, spiritual healing, and hands-on healing such Reiki, acupuncture, and chiropractic.

Although energy therapy comes in many different forms, they all address the energy patterns that evolve in your life. They can positively affect your energy field by helping you tap into higher levels of energy, or frequencies, where your body is able to heal itself. Through the powerful energy therapy modalities, energy is harnessed from a higher level of human functioning to restore balance and help us to be well.

You can experience energy balancing sessions in-person or remotely. Energy balancing is not bound by time and space, and can be effective whether it is done in the same room or remotely, even from a different country.

The Innerlight Method

The Innerlight Method is unique in that it allows energetically sensitive people to function normally in the world. Once they are energetically balanced and understand how to manage their energetic field, they no longer suffer from the common symptoms that arise from being energetically imbalanced. This allows them to continue to lead a normal and active life.

Typically, intuitive people experience one to three Innerlight Method sessions over the course of four to six weeks, and their problems or behaviors diminish significantly or are resolved completely. (Note: There are also other sources of imbalance. Energy balancing can often help with these as well, and in some cases, additional help is required for a person to resume normal functions.)

As I mentioned throughout this book, although the Innerlight Method was initially designed and used with children, adults quickly asked to receive private sessions as well. Caregivers and others in helping professions frequently benefit greatly from learning the Innerlight Method. Caregiver burnout is very common because people who are naturally empathic tend to choose these professions. Some examples of caregiver professions are healers, social workers, therapists, doctors, nurses, psychiatrists, teachers, ministers, and public speakers, to name a few. They often suffer symptoms of feeling nauseated, sick, or exhausted after working with people without understanding why. The Innerlight Method is extremely helpful for this population.

Clearing Your Field with an Innerlight Session

You can receive a private Innerlight Method session from a certified Innerlight Method practitioner who will work intuitively with your energy field so you can access your inner wisdom and enhance your body, mind, and spirit balance.

Innerlight Method practitioners are trained to engage in an intuitive conversation with your higher consciousness to identify areas of imbalance or blockage, and guide you to healing solutions. They can help you learn to balance, manage, and regulate your energetic sensitivities for improved daily living . . . essentially helping you heal yourself.

The Innerlight Method assesses four systems to address imbalances and energetic overload. These systems are:

- The physical body, including the brain, nervous system, digestive system, and endocrine system

- The mental body, including thoughts, beliefs, and emotional patterns
- The spiritual body, which holds your spiritual gifts and destiny
- The energy field itself, including the aura and energetic boundaries

An Innerlight Method session can help you turn down the volume of the energetic/intuitive input you receive to calm your nervous system. This allows you to more fully inhabit your body, improve your focus, increase creative ability, and achieve emotional balance and physical health.

An Innerlight Method session can provide these benefits:

- Bring you into balance with your environment
- Clear blocks caused by stress or trauma
- Clear your field of energy that you are picking up from others
- Identify areas that may need balancing or healing to further personal growth or achieve optimal success and wellness in daily life
- Help you manage your energetic health to prevent future imbalances or blockages

What to Expect in an Energy Balancing Therapy Session

A typical session begins with a brief conversation with your practitioner to discuss the challenges you may be experiencing at home or at school. This allows them to connect with your energy, which informs them of the areas that need to be balanced. While remaining fully clothed, you are invited to lie down on a comfortable massage table and relax. During a remote session, you will be invited to lie on your own sofa or bed.

Most of our clients, especially young children, find this to be a calming, relaxing, and almost meditative process. It is not unusual to have a client drift off into a sleeping state. Initial sessions are usually fifty minutes in length.

At the end of the session, the practitioner speaks with you to share specific details of what was found in your energy field, and check in with you to find out how you are feeling after the treatment.

When You Experience an Energy Session
- Be open to healing on many (sometimes unexpected) levels, rather than be too attached to a particular goal or outcome.
- Drink a lot of water with freshly squeezed lemon after the session to help remove any toxins that may have been released.
- Give yourself a few hours to rest after the treatment to allow energy alignment and integration to occur naturally.
- If the body requires sleep, please rest as much as possible for the remainder of the day and into the next morning.
- Please don't compare your results to another's experience as every session is unique and outcomes cannot be guaranteed.

I do hope that you've gained significant knowledge from reading this book to better handle your intuitive gifts.

For more information on how the Innerlight Method works, I invite you to visit my website at www.innerlightsanctuary.com.

About the Author

Niki Elliott, PhD, is an energy therapist, speaker, author, and pioneer in the fields of energetic healing, holistic education, and intuition development. Niki is the author of *The Intuitive Mother: A 21-Day Journey That Will Change Your Family Forever.*

Through her company, Innerlight Sanctuary, Niki specializes in supporting empathic, intuitive, and highly sensitive children and adults. She trains educators, mental health professionals, and parents to meet the unique needs of this population. She developed the Innerlight Method™ to offer a practical system of energetic healing to help children and adults expand their understanding of energy and intuition. Her greatest joy is watching her clients embrace their highest potential in every area of life through expanding consciousness.

Niki earned a bachelor's degree from UC Berkeley, a master's degree in Curriculum and Instruction from Teachers College, Columbia University, and a PhD in Education from UCLA. As a former elementary school teacher and administrator, Niki helps teachers integrate energy principles in school settings. She trained for more than a decade in energy healing modalities including Usui Reiki, Theta Healing, and Kundalini Yoga. Niki is in demand as an inspirational New Thought speaker. She speaks regularly at the Unity Burbank Center for Spiritual Awareness and other spiritual communities throughout the Southern California region and beyond. She resides with her family in Pasadena, CA.

More information on Niki's workshops, private sessions, and speaking schedule is available at www.InnerlightSanctuary.com.

References

Introduction: Going Down the Rabbit Hole

1. Taylor, J.B., *My Stroke of Insight: A Brain Scientist's Personal Journey*, New York, Plume, 2009.

2. Alexander, E., *Proof of Heaven: A Neurosurgeon's Journey into the Afterlife*, New York, Simon and Schuster, 2012.

3. Brennan, B., *Hands of Light: A Guide to Healing Through the Human Energy Field*, New York, Bantam, 1988.

4. Orloff, J., *Second Sight: An Intuitive Psychiatrist Tells Her Extraordinary Story and Shows You How to Tap into Your Own Inner Wisdom*, New York, Harmony, 2010.

5. Sugrue, T., *There is a River: The Story of Edgar Cayce*, Virginia Beach, A.R.E. Press, 1997.

6. Stein, D., *Essential Reiki: A Complete Guide to an Ancient Healing Art*, Berkeley, Crossing Press, 1995.

7. Khalsa, S., *Kundalini Yoga: The Flow of Eternal Power*, New York, Tarcher Perigree, 1998.

8. Blumenthal, K., *Steve Jobs: The Man Who Thought Different*, New York, Square Fish, 2012.

Chapter 1: Face Your Fear

1. Schwartz, S., *Opening to the Infinite*, Virginia Beach, Nemoseen Media, 2007.

Chapter 2: Identify Your Intuitive Gifts

1. Dale, C., *The Intuition Guidebook*, Minneapolis, Deeper Well Publishing, 2011.
2. Aron, E., *The Highly Sensitive Child: Helping Children Thrive When the World Overwhelms Them*, London, Element, 1999.
3. Ruiz, D.M., *The Fifth Agreement: A Practical Guide to Self-Mastery*, San Rafael, Amber Allen Publishing, 2011.

Chapter 3: Claim Your Power

1. Davis, R. and Braun, E. *The Gift of Learning: Proven New Methods for Correcting ADD, Math & Handwriting Problems*, New York, Tarcher Perigree, 2003.

Chapter 4: Find Your Community

1. Orloff, J., Positive Energy: 10 Extraordinary Prescriptions for Transforming Fatigue, Stress, and Fear into Vibrance, Strength, and Love, New York, Harmony, 2005.
2. Wiseman, S., Writing the Divine: How to Use Channeling for Soul Growth and Healing, Create Space Independent Publishing, 2009.

3. Myss, C., Sacred Contracts: Awakening Your Divine Potential, New York, Harmony, 2003.

Chapter 5: Clear Your Field

1. Eden, D., *Energy Medicine: Balancing Your Body's Energies for Optimal Health, Joy and Vitality*, New York, Jeremy P. Tarcher, 2008.
2. Gerber, R., *Vibrational Medicine: The #1 Handbook of Subtle Energy Therapies*, Vermont, Bear and Co., 2001.
3. Dale, C., *Energy Boundaries: How to Stay Protected and Connected in Work, Love and Life*, Colorado, Sounds True, 2011.

Chapter 6: Practice Energy Hygiene

1. Chodron, P., *How To Meditate: A Practical Guide to Making Friends with Your Mind*, Colorado, Sounds True, 2013.
2. Villodo, A., *One Spirit Medicine: Ancient Ways to Ultimate Wellness*, Carlsbad, Hay House, 2016.
3. Bhajan, Y., *Owner's Manual for the Human Body: Kundalini Yoga as Taught by Yogi Bhajan*, New Mexico, Kundalini Research Institute, 2014.

Chapter 7: Balance Your Intuition and Intellect

1. Berne, V. and Radunsky, V., *On a Beam of Light: A Story of Albert Einstein*, San Francisco, Chronicle Books, 2016.

11126645R00119

Printed in Great Britain
by Amazon